Annett Wolter

Cockatiels

Everything about Acquisition, Care, Nutrition, and Diseases

Translated by Rita and Robert Kimber
Edited by Dr. Matthew M. Vriends

With Color Photographs by Outstanding
Animal Photographers
and Drawings by Fritz W. Köhler

Barron's
Woodbury, New York • London • Toronto • Sydney

First English language edition published in 1984 by
Barron's Educational Series, Inc.
© 1983 (Second edition) by Gräfe und Unzer GmbH,
Munich, West Germany
The title of the German edition is *Nymphensittiche.*

All inquiries should be addressed to:
Barron's Educational Series, Inc.
113 Crossways Park Drive
Woodbury, New York 11797

Library of Congress Catalog Card No. 84-18601

International Standard Book No. 0-8120-2889-9

Library of Congress Cataloging in Publication Data
Wolter, Annette.
   Cockatiels.

   Translation of Nymphensittiche.
   Includes Index.
   1. Cockatiel.   I. Vriends, Matthew M. 1937-
II. Title.
SG473.C6W6513   1984   636.6'865   84-18601
ISBN 0-8120-2889-9

PRINTED IN HONG KONG

23456   490   98765432

Front cover: Two cockatiels, one with natural coloration, the other a lutino.
Inside front cover: A gray male cockatiel with excep-
tionally good colors
Inside back cover: A pair of cockatiels chatting in
domestic tranquility. Note the less brilliant color of the
female's ear coverts (right).
Back cover: (Above left) A gray or normal cockatiel in
flight. (Above right) A lutino in threatening stance.
(Below) Toni and Wutzi nibbling some spray millet.

Photographs
Bielfeld: p. 9; p. 10.
Coleman/Taylor & Burton: p. 53.
Fischer: p. 54.
Reinhard: inside front cover; back cover, above left.
Wothe: front cover; back cover, above right, below; p.
27; p. 28; p. 63; p. 64.

Contents

Preface

I like birds better than any other kind of creature, and of all birds, parrots are my favorites. That is why I said yes without a moment's hesitation when somebody once asked me to look after a cockatiel. An emergency had supposedly come up for the bird's owner, forcing him to leave town at once. The owner didn't return to pick up the bird, whose name was Koko, and I have never heard from the owner again. But since that time Koko has enriched my life and has contributed to my understanding and appreciation of the lovable qualities of cockatiels, their agreeable nature, and their unusual talents.

In my early days with Koko, people who claimed to know about birds bombarded me with "good advice." This advice ranged from suggested food rations, limiting the bird's drinking water, and not offering it any fresh foods to the suggestions that I grab hold of it every day to tame it and that I have its tongue operated on so that it would learn to talk. Fortunately, I disregarded most of these recommendations and relied instead on my own observations and experience with budgerigars.

I acquired Koko years ago, and since then I have gotten to know many cockatiels. My first impressions of these birds were confirmed, and through extensive correspondence with other aviarists and in conversations with veterinarians and breeders I have acquired much detailed information on the proper way of keeping and caring for cockatiels, the diseases they are subject to, and much more. All that I have learned over these many years is summarized in this book. I have tried to bring up everything that might give rise to problems if you have a cockatiel in your home. My discussion of everyday matters like the proper cage, suitable food, and the right way to treat a bird is meant to counter much misinformation that passes as advice. But I also deal in depth with situations that are less likely to occur, such as illness, first aid in case of accidents, and problems that may arise if you have other pets as well. For those who would like to keep a pair of birds and raise their offspring, I describe what to watch out for in breeding and how to set up everything for the birds to raise a family. And since every friend of cockatiels should know as much as possible about the behavior of these birds and how they live in their native habitat in Australia, I have provided information on these topics in the special chapter "Understanding Cockatiels."

I hope that the advice in this book will be well received by friends of cockatiels and that consequently many birds will live happier lives thanks to the better understanding their owners will have acquired and the greater interest they will take in their pets.

Annette Wolter

Short Introduction to Cockatiels

Where do Cockatiels Belong in the Classification of Parrots?

The scientific name for the cockatiel is *Nymphicus hollandicus,* which places this bird with the species parakeets of the group Platycercini within the subfamily Psittacinae. Some ornithologists believe, however, that the cockatiel should be grouped with the cockatoos (subfamily Cacatuinae). No matter which school of thought one goes along with, there is no doubt that cockatiels belong to the family of parrots.

There are a number of features that do support the classification of cockatiels with cockatoos. One of them is the pointed crest that is characteristic of both kinds of birds. The prominent orange coloration of the ear coverts also has an equivalent in some cockatoos. The most startling similarity, however, lies in the brooding behavior of the two kinds of birds. Male cockatiels as well as male cockatoos share the brooding duty with the females, something that is almost unique among all other Australian parakeets and parrots.

On the other hand there is also convincing evidence for assigning cockatiels to the Platycercini, which comprises rosellas and allies. The overall appearance of the cockatiel conforms to this type of bird. And there are some reports, though none of them verified to absolute satisfaction, of cockatiels being crossed with some other members of the Platycercini tribe. If proven correct, these reports would indeed provide powerful evidence because only very closely related species can interbreed and produce offspring.

As already mentioned above, cockatiels definitely belong to the family of parrots, and you will find a simplified classification scheme for the cockatiel on page 49.

How Cockatiels Came to Europe

Australia, the continent with the most varied collection of birds, is also the home of the cockatiel. Cockatiels live there in groups of about 12 birds, but sometimes in larger groups of up to several hundred, primarily in the interior of the continent. In recent years, however, they have also been observed closer to the coast, having been drawn there by the wheat fields. Because of their nomadic way of life, cockatiels have not developed any subspecies.

Figure 1   *Cockatiels can move in all sorts of ways and are truly acrobatic climbers; their heads swivel 180 degrees.*

The first scientist to study cockatiels was Johann Friedrich Gmelin (1746–1804), who described these birds in his revision of the 13th edition of Linné's *Systema Naturae.* Gmelin gave the bird its first name, "Cockatoo Parrot" *(Psittacus novaehollandiae).* Unfortunately we have no idea who first added the "nymphicus" to the name, though when we look at the slender shape of the bird, its graceful movements and bright but not gaudy coloring, the association to nymphs, the nature goddesses of Greek mythology, seems quite appropriate and understandable.

Short Introduction to Cockatiels

In the early eighteenth century some sailors brought cockatiels home from Australia to England, but the chance of survival for these imported birds was very slim. A strict ban on the export of native birds issued by the Australian government in 1894 proved to be a great boon. Not only did it protect many wild species of birds from extinction but it also made the birds already living in captivity more precious, indeed, irreplaceable. Now they had to be kept under conditions that not just ensured their survival but also were conducive to producing offspring. The first successes in breeding cockatiels in captivity came in the latter half of the nineteenth century, and since that time hardly any cockatiels that were born in the wild have been brought to Europe. The first successful brood was registered in the United States in 1910.

Natural Coloration and Variations

For a long time the appearance of the cockatiels raised in captivity remained the same. As in their Australian ancestors, the ground color of the plumage is a delicate gray which sometimes has a more bluish and sometimes a more brownish tinge. The upper tail coverts are a silvery gray, and the lower tail coverts dark gray to black. White feathers on the outer coverts provide a striking contrast on the wings. The throat, cheeks, and forehead are a pure lemon yellow, and in this yellow mask the bright orange ear coverts stand out conspicuously underneath the black eyes. The row of crest feathers rises from the yellow forehead. The shorter front feathers of the crest are yellow, the longer back ones gray like the crown but with some yellow barbs mingled in. The crest of a cockatiel is considerably slimmer than that of a cockatoo and less mobile. From the sides of the brownish ceres a faint line of small gray feathers runs to the eyes, separating the upper half of the mask with its more vivid yellow from the lower half with its fainter color, which often fades to almost white toward the chin.

The plumage of the two sexes differs somewhat, with the female showing less of a color contrast and having yellow and black crossbarring on the under tail coverts.

The juvenile plumage is like that of the adult female but does include the striking color pattern of the under tail coverts. After the first adult molt, which is completed between the fourth and the ninth month, it is easy to tell males from females by the relative intensity of the colors. By that time the bill is dark gray to blackish gray or brown as in the adult birds, and the legs have become a dark blue gray.

Breeders of cockatiels felt the urge to try to achieve modifications in the natural plumage of their birds, and by applying Mendel's laws of heredity they succeeded in changing the appearance of some cockatiels.

- The most striking result of their efforts is the **albino,** which is basically white but retains the yellow mask with the orange ear coverts. In male albinos the lower tail feathers are a pale yellow, and in the female they are a bright yellow. Albinos have light gray feet and red eyes and look like miniature Sulphur-Crested Cockatoos.
- The results of other crossings also have a basically white plumage but with pale yellow shadings. These birds have large, black eyes. Because of their black eyes, they look even more stunning than the regulr albinos, but they are not pure albinos.
- In the lingo of breeders, albinos that are basically white but have an even, delicate, yellow cast all over are called **lutinos** (from *luteus,* the Latin word for yellow).
- There are also **pearled** cockatiels. Their coloration is lighter than that of the wild strain (gray or normal), and there are clear white or yellow dots on the wing coverts. On the lower back and the sides these dots are somewhat blurred. The tail feathers of these pearled cockatiels are a brilliant gold or silver with black bands. This mutation occurs with both red and black eyes.

Short Introduction to Cockatiels

• The so-called **laced** cockatiels look like the pearled variant, but each feather has a dark or light rim.

• Apart from the color mutations already mentioned, there are **pied** cockatiels in different combinations of colors. These birds have clearly delineated patches of other-colored feathers — pearled, laced, or unicolored — that stand out against the ground color. A number of different variants are bred, such as the **head pied,** the **heavy pied,** and the **cinnamon pied.**

• Breeders have also succeeded in producing a "**black**" cockatiel. The basic color of this cockatiel is not pitch black, to be sure; but the dark slate color forms an impressive contrast to the yellow head with its orange ear coverts and to the white on the wings.

• Another color variant is **cinnamon.**

• Well-known are the **silver** cockatiels with a ground color that has been refined to a light silver tone and with contrasting patches of the various other colors.

In my opinion, all these innovations should not be overvalued, attractive as they may be. After all, they represent nothing more than the manipulation and deliberate crossing of genes. And experience tells us that the products of complex inbreeding are much more susceptible to diseases than birds with naturally colored plumage or with simple color mutations.

Figure 2   *Having its head gently scratched is bliss for a cockatiel — as long as it is in the mood for it.*

Considerations Before You Buy

Before you set out to buy a cockatiel from a breeder or a pet shop, you should seriously ask yourself some questions.

Does a Bird Fit In with Your Way of Life?

A cockatiel is the right pet for you only if you can answer the following questions honestly and in good conscience with a yes.

1. Are you aware that cockatiels are by nature gregarious, loyal, and intelligent creatures that need either a partner of their own kind – if kept singly – or a person (i.e., you) as a substitute partner? A cockatiel that is left alone too much suffers from loneliness and boredom and may become neurotic or physically ill.

2. If you have a job and are away from home more than six hours a day, is another member of the household who is willing to spend some time with the bird at home either all the time or at least several hours a day?

3. Do you have children or other members of the family who are both willing and able to pay attention to the bird?

4. If there is nobody who has enough time for the bird, are you willing to set up the room where the bird lives properly and safely for it and supply it with appropriate toys? (For details on safety, consult the list of dangers on pp. 33–34.)

5. Or, if time is a problem, would you be willing to buy a pair of birds and a sufficiently spacious cage for them?

6. Can you live with some dirt? Cockatiels are not and cannot be house-trained. They leave behind droppings wherever they sit, they shed feathers, especially fine down, and they shake dust out of their plumage. They also drop bits of food and break branches into wood chips. You have to put up with all of this and not try to teach the bird better manners.

7. Do you like to spend your nonwork time at home? If you like to go out a lot and spend weekends away from home, will you still have enough hours and patience left to devote to your bird?

8. Will you be able to provide first-class care for your cockatiel when you have to spend time away from home (p. 43)?

9. Are you aware that although most cockatiels can learn to say a few words and whistle some melodies, very few develop a great talent for speech? Will you be fond of your cockatiel even if its talents are only modest?

Taking Responsibility for the Life of a Bird

Before you set out to buy a bird, remember that you are about to take on the responsibility for a living creature. Have you considered the following points?

• Surprising someone with a gift cockatiel is not always a good idea. The lucky person might have preferred to decide for himself whether or not to be responsible for a bird for anywhere from ten to fifteen years.

• Cockatiels do not make good Christmas presents. A young bird that is accustomed to the cozy warmth of a nest or a pet shop should not be transported during cold or – worse yet – wet and cold weather.

• A cockatiel is not an appropriate gift for small children. Children like to play with their presents, which they cannot do with a shy bird. Children also like to pet and pick up animals. Cockatiels should therefore be given only to older children and only if the parents are willing to take over the care for the bird when the child's interest begins to flag.

Cockatiels and Other Pets

I know several dog owners who also keep cockatiels. The coexistence of these two kinds of animals is possible only if the dog is good-natured and obeys its master's every word. The dog will have to learn to overcome its hunting instinct and

Plate 2   *Some of the loveliest color variations.*
Above: *Silver cockatiel and pied cockatiel.*
Below: *Cockatiel with natural coloration (gray or normal) and pearled cockatiel.*

conquer its feelings of jealousy toward the feathered newcomer. It will have to respond reliably and in all situations to the repeated no it hears in connection with the bird. As long as the bird stays in its cage, it is safe enough. But when the bird is let loose in the house, the dog's obedience may be severely tested if, for instance, the bird approaches the dog curiously, lands on the dog's back, or dares to approach its food dish. Make sure the two are left together for any length of time only in your presence. Then, if such situations arise, you can assuage the dog's jealousy or hunting instinct with persuasive talk. Once the dog has accepted the bird as a member of its "pack," excessive caution is no longer necessary.

I strongly advise you, however, not to keep a cat and a bird together in the same house. Cats remain cats and fierce predators. This is true in spite of occasional stories of friendships that are said to have developed between felines and birds.

You should also avoid keeping unconfined rabbits or guinea pigs in the same room with a bird. The bird might frighten these rodents, and if they feel threatened they may defend themselves or their territory against the bird. Since, unlike dogs, they do not develop inhibitions or respect for pack members, they may bite and scratch or even kill the bird.

But you can keep cockatiels easily with other birds in a room without restrictions. Cockatiels get along well with budgerigars, canaries, Java sparrows, siskins, Australian grass parakeets, lovebirds, weavers, and many exotic finches. The only thing you have to watch out for is to separate breeding pairs because cockatiels take such a great interest in this business that they are a nuisance and can disrupt smaller nesting birds. Conversely, you should protect a brooding pair of cockatiels against interference from birds of other species. Of course, birds of different kinds first have to adjust to the community and should stay in individual cages until they have had a chance to get acquainted through the bars with the other birds and are ready to join them in the flying area.

What You May Expect from Your Cockatiel

If your cockatiel was born in captivity it is used to humans and to living in a confined space. Once it has adjusted to its new home, it will delight you with its pretty appearance and tameness. You will enjoy watching how it gets more and more comfortable in its surroundings, learns to understand certain routines, and often acquires some amusing habits of its own. You will also be quite amazed how your bird will gradually learn to communicate to you what it likes and dislikes and what it is afraid of. It will approach you more and more, take part in your activities, and vie for your attention and favors. Soon you will receive – and learn to interpret (pp. 55–56) – signs of great affection, expressed in cockatiel fashion.

Cockatiels, like many parrots, have the ability to learn to speak. But their major talent is in imitating the voices of our songbirds and in repeating simple melodies and other sounds. Still, I know some cockatiels that can say their own names, produce short sentences, and infallibly say "good morning" when their owners first enter the room. Their gift for speech is not as impressive as that of mynahs, African gray parrots, or budgerigars. But if you are patient enough and repeat words and short sentences often enough, your cockatiel may repeat them someday. On the other hand it is just possible that your bird has neither the talent nor the inclination for speaking. This should be no reason for disappointment; it does not indicate that the bird is any less intelligent.

Cockatiels do not match African gray parrots, cockatoos, macaws, or amazons in intelligence. In this respect the species just mentioned are unequaled in the world of birds, but they are also as demanding of care and affection as babies. Cockatiels rank considerably higher in intelligence than songbirds, pigeons, and quite a few mammals. Their abilities and performance are perhaps best compared to those of budgerigars.

Considerations Before You Buy

A Single Bird or a Pair?

A pair is always appropriate if the birds are intended to provide company for an older or a handicapped person who spends a lot of time alone or for a child who tends to feel lonely. A pair is also the right choice if you are primarily interested in watching the birds and enjoying their lively presence and not so much in developing a close relationship with your pets. Pairs are less likely to learn to talk than single birds! If it seems likely that nobody in the family will have the time or the inclination in the long run to pay a lot of attention to a bird, then the only possibility is a pair of birds.

But be aware from the very outset that a pair of birds, particularly if they are constantly or almost constantly confined to a cage, require considerably more space than a single bird that is part of the family and spends hours or even days at a time unrestrained in a room or apartment. The ideal setup for pair of cockatiels is a room-sized aviary that contains not only a few perches and the necessary items for feeding but also a climbing tree constructed of natural branches. Keeping two birds in an aviary large enough to allow for at least limited exercise of the flight muscles is the most humane solution for keeping birds in captivity.

If you want to have the best of both worlds — i.e., you would like to watch a pair of birds but after some time have some close personal contact with them — you should muster patience and first take the time to build up a friendship between you and a single bird and only then buy a second bird. The newcomer will at first focus all its attention on the other bird and regard you more with timidity than interest. But this initially shy bird will learn quite quickly, given the example of its partner, how useful humans can be. And since it will be eager to share all the habits and activities of its partner, the day will come when the two will actually compete for the favorite perch on your shoulder or for getting first turn at having their heads scratched. In addition, you will have the pleasure of observing and getting insights into the "marital life" and perhaps even the "family life" of the birds.

Male or Female?

The question of whether to get a male or a female bird is of concern only if you are interested in breeding birds. If kept singly, males and females adapt equally well to a new home and to a human partner. Neither sex is more intelligent or more likely to talk or whistle.

Since the most obvious difference between a gray-colored (or normal) male and female cockatiel lies in the brightness of the plumage, the best way to tell the sex is to see adult birds of both sexes next to each other. More than one cockatiel has been thought by its owner to be a male until the day it laid an egg. You will not even realize your mistake if you want a pair and inadvertently purchase two birds of the same sex. If two cockatiels of the same sex are kept together in captivity, one of them will gradually assume the role of the opposite sex.

Pairs of cockatiels never quarrel seriously or fight. Problems are likely to arise only when you introduce a third bird. The false marriage between the two original birds will dissolve if the newcomer is of the opposite sex. The female who has been playing the dominant role up to this point will now lay claim to the true sexual partner, who, however, may be more interested in the other female. Now the previously happy couple turns into a pair of rivals. Although even this situation is unlikely to spark physical aggression, the loser will have to lead the lonely life of a bystander. It is therefore better to have four birds. If you can keep only three, make sure they are of the same sex. Two of them will form a close friendship, but they will at least not regard the third one as a rival.

Buying a Bird

Where to Find Healthy Birds

There are three routes to acquiring a young, healthy cockatiel:
- You can buy one at a pet store.
- You can buy one from a breeder.
- You can be given a bird because a pair of cockatiels owned by someone you know has produced offspring.

Never purchase a bird from a catalog through a mail-order company. If you do, you have no chance to actually see and choose your bird, and you have to accept whatever comes. In addition, the bird will be bewildered and traumatized on arrival so that you will not be able to tell until later if there is something wrong with it. You will not be able to simply return an animal that is sick and still in a state of shock from the ordeal of shipping it has just undergone. If there is neither a breeder nor a pet store carrying birds near you, try the nearest larger town, or put an ad in the paper.

Have a good look at the pet store where you intend to purchase your bird. Are the birds kept in large enough cages, or are they crowded together? Do they have fresh food and water? Are the cages clean and is there fresh sand on the bottom? Do the birds get enough air and light? If there is any question in your mind, it is better not to take the risk of acquiring a sick bird. If you buy from a breeder, you can generally do so in full confidence because his birds would not reproduce if they did not receive proper care. Neither a breeder nor a conscientious dealer will try to palm off an old bird on you instead of a young one, let alone sell you a sick bird.

How to Tell If a Bird Is Healthy

Here are a few points to look out for:
- Is the bird that appeals to you hopping around the cage actively, eating, grooming itself, interacting with others of its species, or watching with interest what is going on outside the cage? If it is sitting quietly in a corner with puffed-up feathers, this may, but does not necessarily, indicate illness. Cockatiels sometimes nap during the day. But it is safer to observe such a quiet bird a little longer to get a chance to see it in its period of activity.

Figure 3   *Typical sleeping posture of a cockatiel: The bill is tucked into the slightly raised back feathers, and the eyes are closed. If the bird is sleeping soundly, one leg is often hidden in the feathers of the abdomen.*

- Look not only at the colors but also at the consistency of the bird's plumage. A young and healthy cockatiel has shiny feathers that lie down smoothly on the body. The feathers near the cloaca should not be dirty, because this is a sign of diarrhea.
- The eyes of a young cockatiel should be shiny, large, round, and black. In the case of an albino they are red.
- Also examine the legs. They should be straight and clean, the toes perfectly shaped, and the toenails not too long. The horny scales on the legs and feet should be smooth and even.
- Once you have made your choice, the bird is grabbed with a gentle but secure grip (Figure 4) and removed from the cage. If the bird nips the dealer's hand, this is nothing more than a sign of the bird's energy and health. While the dealer is

13

Buying a Bird

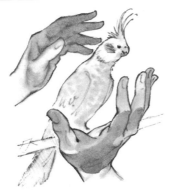

Figure 4 *The safest method of catching a bird: One hand reaches for the back from above and the other is placed against the belly.*

still holding the bird, check the feathers around the anus once more. Ask the salesperson to blow against the feathers of this region so that you can see if the skin underneath is red, which might be a sign of disease. Run your finger over the sternum to make sure it is rounded. A convex sternum also indicates disease.

The Band

Before the bird is placed in the box for you to take home, look at the numbered band on its foot. This band proves that the bird comes from an aviculturist who is a member of a cockatiel society. The number on the band is registered both by the breeder and the society.

Since it is usually not possible to enter cockatiels in an exhibition unless they have been ringed (banded), it is necessary to know something about this procedure. The best time to ring your cockatiels is when they are seven to ten days old. (There is no set time for this, because it depends on the speed with which the chicks grow; young that are fed well grow faster than those that are not.)

Blacken the ring by holding it over a burning candle, as shiny rings will sometimes lead to anxiety; the parents birds will often want to remove the ring from the nest and whether there is a young bird attached to this shining "thing" does not really make any difference.

The band is first pushed over the two front toes, which have been "glued" together with vaseline; then the two back toes are "glued" to the leg, after which the ring is pushed further. Clean the foot after ringing. The banding of cockatiels should take place in the evening, as the parents' urge to keep the nest clean has been lessened somewhat.

Ringing a bird is not as easy as it looks, but once you have done it a few times it should no longer present any problems. Rings can be ordered through a cockatiel fanciers' association or club (see page 61) with which you are affiliated. The appropriate ring size for cockatiels is 1/5 inch in diameter.

What a Cockatiel Needs for Its Well-Being

Once you have reached the decision that you would like to have a cockatiel, go out and buy the right kind of cage and all the accessories your bird will need from the very first day on. Your new pet will be confused and frightened by the change in its life and by the trip and should have the chance to get acquainted right away with the setting that will become its new home, namely, a well-equipped cage.

The Right Cage

A cage a bird will spend much of its time in can never be more than a poor substitute environment, but this substitute should be as humane as possible and offer the cockatiel at least shelter and a sense of safety and comfort. The frequently heard statement that cockatiels should have enough room in a cage to fly at least a short span is nonsense. Anyone who has seen a cockatiel fly free knows that no cage and not even most outdoor aviaries are large enough to accommodate these birds which fly straight as an arrow. Nevertheless, a cockatiel should be able to move around in its cage without constantly running into perches or the grating of the cage. It has to be able to fully extend its wings sideways and upward without bumping into anything, and there has to be enough room between the individual perches and in front of the food dishes. For a single bird this means that the cage has to be *at least* 24 inches (60 cm) long, 16 inches (40 cm) tall, and 14 inches (35 cm) deep. If you buy a larger cage, you give your bird more freedom of movement and may later introduce a partner into the setting it is already familiar with.

The walls of the cage should be made of rust-free metal bars that are sturdy enough to withstand onslaughts by beaks of medium-sized parrots. If possible, the bars on two of the walls should run horizontally so that the bird can climb up and down on them. The metal frame of the cage should stand on a plastic base about 6 inches (15 cm)

deep, which will keep sand and leftover food from being kicked out. A flat plastic tray in this base should move in and out easily to facilitate the changing of the sand at the bottom. Some manufacturers superimpose a metal grate over this plastic tray. It is supposed to keep the bird from stepping on its droppings when approaching the food dishes. But such a grate is impractical not

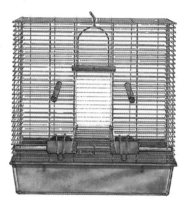

Figure 5 *An excellent solidly built cage with the minimum dimensions 24 × 15 × 14 inches (60 × 40 × 35 cm).*

only because the droppings obviously land on it, too, but primarily because it interferes with the bird's picking up sand, which is important for the bird's digestion and as a source of mineral elements. Also, cockatiels sometimes like to walk on the bottom and pick up seeds, as they often do in nature. I therefore recommend that you remove such a floor grate if the cage you are buying is equipped with one. You will save yourself an additional cleaning chore and make life a little more comfortable for your bird.

Important: The containers for seeds and water are usually attached to the base of the cage. Make sure that the space above the water dish, especially, is clear. Cockatiels drink by picking up

15

drops of water in their beaks, lifting their heads high, and letting the liquid run down their throats into the crop. To make sure food and water are not contaminated by droppings, place the perches in such a way that the bird never sits directly over the dishes.

Choose a plain cage, rectangular in shape and without ornaments like arches, turrets, and bays. These elaborate shapes only take up space and provide occasion for injuries. Wooden parts would meet your cockatiel's approval because it could indulge its love for gnawing on them, but they would soon be ruined and the cage would no longer be escape-proof. You are better off not buying a round cage, because such cages offer no points of reference and birds do not feel really safe and comfortable in them. If you already have a round cage, place a mirror or a forked branch in it as an aid to orientation.

Check how well the gate locks. Cockatiels are smart and strong enough to realize that with a little practice they will be able to open a door that simply snaps shut. The safest solution is to secure the closed cage door with a padlock.

The perches that come with the cage you buy are all of the same diameter, which is detrimental to the leg and foot muscles of the bird. In the wild, birds perch and rest on branches of different thicknesses. Replace the artificial perches of the cage with natural branches, some of which are of the same thickness as the ones you remove while others are a little thicker and thinner. Most of the branches should be thick enough that the toes of the bird do not quite meet (Figure 6). **Avoid poisonous woods** like yew, buckthorn, arbor vitae, oleander, or horsechestnut. Willow, hazelnut, oak, maple, and fruit trees are fine. If you use branches from fruit trees, make sure they have not been sprayed with insecticides. Rinse all branches with hot water and let them dry thoroughly before placing them in the cage, and replace them with new ones from time to time. But do not use so many branches that they interfere with the bird's

moving around the cage. Four or five branches are plenty. If there is a ladder in the cage, remove it because it will only be in the way.

Figure 6   *Perches have to be thick enough that the cockatiel cannot reach all the way around with its toes. (Left: Correct diameter. Right: A perch that is too thin.)*

The Right Spot for the Cage

Pick the spot for the cage before your cockatiel arrives. Your bird needs a permanent location where it feels at home and to which it can retreat. The room where it is going to live should have an even temperature that remains around 66°–70°F (19°–21°C) in the winter. A dark corner is just as unsuitable for its cage as is a place in front of a window where the sun beats in for hours at a time. Birds need light and air, but hot sunshine from which there is no escape can lead to heatstroke, and if there is too little light, they lose their vitality. Choose a spot near a window and make sure there are no leaks around the window frame. Birds catch cold easily from cold air that enters through cracks or from drafts caused by open doors and windows. The ideal place for the cage should be light and draft-free and not in the middle of family traffic, but also not so far out of the way that the bird cannot observe what is going on in the room. The cage should be high enough that there are no activities taking place above it; and its back should be up against a wall to give the bird a sense of safety.

All loud noises are frightening to birds and will in the long run make them nervous and jumpy. That is why the cage should not be close to the telephone, radio, or TV. The sound and picture of

What a Cockatiel Needs for Its Well-Being

a TV do not bother a bird if they are not too close, but remote-control switches are harmful because they work by ultrasonic sound, and these sound waves are extremely unpleasant to the sensitive hearing organs of birds. Other unsuitable locations for a bird cage are next to the refrigerator or the dishwasher, because their humming and vibrating also scare birds. The kitchen in general is a poor place for a bird because cooking vapors and especially smoking fat and changes in temperature caused by a hot stove and subsequent airing are unhealthy for birds and can make them sick. If the cockatiel has to share the living space of a smoker, it is absolutely essential that the room where the bird cage is located be aired thoroughly but without creating drafts several times a day and especially in the evening before bedtime. If you occasionally have guests who smoke and a blue cloud hovers in the air, you might consider moving the bird cage to another room at these occasions. A bird that has lived with you long enough to feel comfortable and at home will take such a change in stride, but make sure the other room has the same temperature because cockatiels react strongly to sudden fluctuations in warmth.

Living Area: Climbing Tree, Bird Room

Important as a good cage and the proper location for it are, they do not provide a real living area for a cockatiel. A cage is the place to which it likes to retreat for resting and eating or for observing the goings-on with a mixture of apprehension and curiosity. But when a cockatiel is in an active mood it needs more freedom of movement than a cage can offer; it would like to fly, climb, gnaw, and keep busy. Normally this need is satisfied if the bird has certain periods when it can fly free in the room. It will then make for its favorite perches, a lamp, perhaps, or a bookcase or a curtain rod. There it will sit for a while and amuse itself. On a piece of furniture it can trip back and

forth, and on a curtain rod or lamp it can do acrobatics upside down, but after a while it will start picking at the material of the curtains or the lampshade or at the wire of the lamp, none of which will please you.

You may also be less than enthusiastic when the first dropping descend from a high perch to the floor or leave their mark somewhere else. Actually the droppings are not too serious; either you can remove them right away with a tissue and wipe the spot with a moist paper towel, or you can let them dry and then brush or vacuum them off. The beak marks on furniure and other objects, on the other hand, cannot be removed and become more and more unsightly with time. The only thing to do is to sacrifice a few objects that the cockatiel can gradually destroy and that you then replace with new ones that will go the same route. If you distribute these objects around the room in the bird's favorite spots, it will keep busy with them and leave everything else pretty much alone. The furnishings of the room are in least danger if there is a climbing tree (Figure 7) next to your cockatiel's cage.

Figure 7 *A big climbing tree you can assemble yourself. You need a big tub and enough gravel and sand to fill it, as well as a log with some holes drilled in it and three thick branches with bark.*

What a Cockatiel Needs for Its Well-Being

You have to assemble the climbing tree yourself. The simplest way is to set a small tree trunk with branches in a Christmas tree stand or attach it at the bottom to a wooden cross. If you use a tub that is wider than the longest branches reach, anything that gets dropped from the tree falls into the tub. Place a large log in the middle of the tub and drill holes in it into which you fit forked branches. Fill in the bottom of the tub around the log first with gravel and then with soil and top this with a 2-inch (5 cm) layer of bird sand. Then you can remove all the droppings and debris in a matter of seconds with a slotted spoon. (There are also ready-to-use climbing trees available at pet stores.) Your cockatiel will live happily with such a climbing tree. Of course, it will chew on the branches and drop them to the ground in little bits, but they can be replaced easily enough. Since cockatiels are real fliers rather than flutterers they refuse to take to the air for short distances, and you should therefore construct a little ramp leading from the cage to the tree so that the bird can climb back and forth easily.

Figure 8 *Cockatiels climb from branch to branch with great dexterity, making use of legs, tail, and bill.*

If you have really spacious living quarters, you can construct an indoor aviary in a light but draft-free corner of a room. Such an indoor aviary is suitable primarily for a pair of cockatiels or for a cockatiel that lives together with one or two budgerigars or zebra finches. Even though a bird lives close to you in an indoor aviary, it cannot share actively enough in your life under these conditions and should therefore not be forced to live alone. The aviary should be large enough for flying from one corner to the opposite one with several flaps of the wings, i.e., 3–4 feet (1–1.5 m) deep and at least 6 feet (2 m) long. It should also be tall enough to allow for easy cleaning and care of the birds.

When setting up an aviary it is important to use the right wire mesh. If you are going to include smaller birds such as budgerigars or tropical finches with your cockatiel, the mesh should be no coarser than 1/2 inches (1 cm). If the setup is for cockatiels only, it should be slightly under 1 inch (2 cm). The birds should not be able to stick their heads through the mesh because if they do they will not be able to pull them back because of the lay of the feathers, and they can easily be strangled.

If you have a male and a female cockatiel, the pair may lay eggs and raise young in an artificial nest. There is hardly a bird lover who would be able to resist the temptation of letting nature take its course under these circumstances. All you need to do is to place nesting boxes in the aviary (pp. 45–46) and in a few weeks the pair will have become a small flock. But the next step is inevitably – for reasons of space – an outdoor aviary.

Cockatiels in Outdoor Aviaries

For instructions on how to build an outdoor aviary (Figure 9) I can only refer you to literature on keeping and breeding cockatiels in aviaries

What a Cockatiel Needs for Its Well-Being

Figure 9   *An indoor aviary provides enough space for several cockatiels or for several birds of different species as well as for nesting boxes.*

because this little book is aimed primarily at bird lovers who want to live in close contact with their birds. It is obvious that birds living in an aviary are not likely to form close bonds with humans because they live together with members of their own or similar species. The role of the human is to take responsibility for their well-being and to protect them from everything that might cause them harm or discomfort. The only thing I should like to say here emphatically is that I disagree with all authorities who claim that cockatiels and budgerigars can be kept year round in an outdoor aviary with an attached unheated shelter area. These authors argue that more protection is unnecessary because the birds survive below-freezing nighttime temperatures in their native habitat. I should like to counter this by pointing out that in Australia nights with below-freezing readings do occur, but that these low temperatures last only for a few hours at a time and never as an extended

cold period. If cockatiels and budgerigars do survive cold spells in unheated shelters, it is indeed survival, mere survival, but not a life that can be enjoyed.

Useful Accessories for Your Bird

There are more toys and other small items available for budgerigars than for any other kind of bird. Unfortunately, these things are not suitable for cockatiels because they do not stand up to the much stronger beak of a cockatiel.

You should definitely look for a special *bathhouse* (Figure 10) for cockatiels, which may be available from the same manufacturer who made the cage. The bathhouse has to be large enough for cockatiels and should be made so it hooks in the open door of the cage. Make sure the bottom has a textured surface because otherwise the

What a Cockatiel Needs for Its Well-Being

Figure 10 *A bathhouse with a textured bottom and glass walls to keep the water from splashing all over. The contraption is designed to be hung in the cage door (available at pet supply stores).*

Figure 11 *A lukewarm shower administered with a spray bottle serves as a substitute for the rain baths that cockatiels get in their natural habitat.*

cockatiel may slip and that would effectively ruin its pleasure and interest in baths. If you regularly – and from the beginning – hand the contraption, filled with about 1 inch (3 cm) of lukewarm water, in the cage, it will gradually get used to this initially frightening object. Leave the thing there for several hours, and at some point the desire for a bath will overcome the initial timidity. From that point on the bird will quite frequently ask for a bath. It will show this by trying to get into the container with the drinking water or by shaking and fluffing its feathers the way it does before entering the water, or it may circle around a glass of water on the table, again with fluffed feathers, or it may follow you to the kitchen or bath and seek out a dripping faucet. If you cannot find a bathhouse, buy a spray bottle for watering plants, and sprinkle your cockatiel on an especially warm summer day with luke-warm water from the bottle held diagonally above it (Figure 11). This resembles the baths cockatiels take in their Australian homeland by sitting on trees when it begins to rain and stretching out their wings and twisting and turning so that the rain falls on all parts of the body. In Australia, cockatiels bathe and drink from puddles and

streams, too, but they are especially fearful and nervous when on the ground. Besides, such oppor-tunities for bathing are quite rare in their native habitat (p. 58). Instead of a spray bottle, you can use a hand-held shower head in your bathroom. Place the cage without the base in the bathtub, and let the lukewarm water sprinkle over part of the cage. This gives the bird a chance to decide whether or not it feels like taking a bath.

Important: Use the spray bottle only for the bird. Double-check to make sure you do not by mistake have the wrong bottle that may have contained pesticides for spraying plants.

When your cockatiel has already become quite trusting and is no longer afraid of you or new objects, try to blow-dry it gently after a bath. Set the dryer at medium and first let the warm air flow by it gently. If it likes it, it will demonstrate its enjoyment by turning slowly and luxuriously. I have known cockatiels to express feelings of anticipatory pleasure at the mere mention of the word "hair dryer" or at hearing the hum of an electric toothbrush in the bathroom.

You also need additional *dishes*. Cages come equipped with a water and a food dish, but this is probably not enough because you will want to give your bird fruit, vegetables, and treats, too. If the cage offers enough room, you can simply put sturdy little dishes you already have on the floor though not directly under a perch. If there is not enough floor area, however, you should buy the largest food containers you can find that can be attached to the horizontal bars of the cage. The best height for them is at the level of the perches. Lettuce leaves, parsley, spray millet, etc., can be held by a clothespin that is attached to the cage, or you can buy a special little rack for them (Figure 12).

Another practical addition to the basic food dishes are automatic *seed and water dispensers.* Buy the largest you can get because cockatiels have to dip their relatively big beaks deep into the water to be able to drink. And the seed dispenser has to be able to handle sunflower seeds without clogging up. Water dispensers are especially practical because the water in them stays clean. Automatic dispensers are also advantageous if the bird occasionally has to be left without a caretaker for a day or two, assuming, of course, that the bird is used to eating and drinking from these devices. Some birds get the hang of it right away. Then there is no problem. But others fail to learn the trick and it has happened that birds died for want of food and water with filled containers right in front of them. So be sure to leave regular food and water dishes in the cage until your bird has gotten used to the self-service ones.

Figure 12   *A rack for greens; can also be used for holding spray millet and pieces of fruit.*

Appropriate Toys

Cockatiels do not play games the way dogs and even many budgerigars who have made friends with people do. Cockatiels are more like large parrots; they want to be busy – i.e., they need the right kind of objects they can work over with their beaks. Give your cockatiel *fresh* branches as often as possible for gnawing, and it will be happily occupied for hours in the most healthy and natural manner. If no branches are available, something like wooden curtain rings will do, or empty yarn spoons, or bast fiber braids or ropes you can make yourself. Pet stores also sell wooden toys for cockatiels.

But your cockatiel will be happiest of all if it is simply allowed to be with you, sitting on your shoulder or on some other close and convenient perch, and watching whatever its human friend is doing. I know a seamstress with a cockatiel whose favorite spot is on her work table. There it patiently runs one pin after the other through its beak, drops it next to the pin box and starts on the next one as though trying to polish each and every pin. This sounds more dangerous than it is. The tongues of the birds are so sensitive and agile that they deal with the pins carefully and cleverly enough. You have to be much more on the alert for poisonous substances, because even brief contact with them can do great harm to the tongue. You have to be especially careful about this because in nature birds have no experience with such substances and have therefore not developed any protective instincts. See to it that the bird has no contact with poisonous woods or house plants, lead or lead alloys, mercury (as from broken thermometers), pesticides, and all kinds of cleansers (pp. 33–34).

What your cockatiel would appreciate is a little *bell* or a *mirror* in its cage. It will not really use them for toys. The bell will serve it as a "second voice," which it will sound when it wants to proclaim that it regards its house as its sole and unlimited property. It will ring it whenever it leaves it or returns to it. Many cockatiels sleep directly under or next to their bell and treat it almost like a member of their flock. The bell should be suspended from a strong, short chain that will not break easily and on which the bird cannot strangle itself. The mirror should be purchased from a pet dealer. You should pick a hanging mirror designed for larger parrots that is made of stainless steel and has no frame. If you choose a different kind, the cockatiel will soon chew through the mounting and might get hurt when the mirror drops to the floor.

By suggesting that a single cockatiel should be given a mirror I find myself in opposition to some articles that have recently appeared in popular magazines. These articles warn against giving cockatiels mirrors because cockatiels can supposedly get sick from seeing their mirror image and being sexually stimulated by it. The theory that cockatiels or other birds can get sick this way is a hypothesis, not a proven fact. It is a fact beyond dispute, however, that caged birds languish because of loneliness and boredom and sometimes die prematurely (especially if they are gregarious, bond for life, and live in flocks the way budgerigars and cockatiels do). If such a bird is kept singly, it turns to its human partner not only for companionship but also out of sexual needs. A mirror will provide comfort for many a lonely hour. Surely it also acts as a sexual stimulus, but a healthy bird remains sexually active and finds substitute objects for courtship displays even without a mirror. You cannot banish all reflecting surfaces from your living room; somewhere the bird will find something shiny that will reflect the bird's image, which will be taken for a companion of its own species. My cockatiel Koko chose the shiny microphone of a dictating machine to serve sometimes as his bride and sometimes as an object to vent his aggression on. The female Lucy used to devotedly feed the glassed-in face of a small standing clock; and Max, a proud lutino, occa-

Figure 13 *Once a cockatiel has been hand-tamed, it will not object to being carried back to its cage.*

sionally attempted to mate with his owner's hairdo. Anyone ranting against the use of mirrors should have the courage of going all the way and object to the keeping of birds in captivity as being against nature. I, personally, find the compromise solution of a mirror acceptable and recommend it.

A Name for Your Cockatiel

Decide early on what you are going to call your cockatiel. If you use the name from the first day on, the bird will soon learn that this word, which it keeps hearing, has something to do with it. The name should be short so that a bird with a gift for speech can repeat it soon. According to my observations, words with the sounds "ah," "ee," or "oo" are easier than others although I have heard cockatiels call out the names Koko, Chiko, and Beppo.

Getting Your Cockatiel to Feel at Home

Arrival in the New Home

When you bring your cockatiel home, its cage should stand ready for it in its permanent location and be equipped with food, water, and sand on the floor. The removal from the cage on the day of the purchase, the trip home, and the new surroundings are all horrible experiences for the bird. It is filled with terror, and its only wish is to get away from human beings and hide in the hole of a tree.

Do not try to get hold of it once more. Simply open the transport cage or box in front of the open cage in such a way that the bird, which will move toward the light, is bound to end up inside the cage. You can count on its wanting to leave behind the transport container, but it might try to climb up the outside of its new cage rather than into it. You can block it by holding your flat hand above its head. In the unlikely event that the bird refuses to budge, tilt the container gently so that the bird slides through the open cage door. If worse comes to worst, lift the top of the cage off the base, place the open transport container on the cage floor, put the top back on the base, and wait, with the cage door closed, until the bird chooses to move out of the container. Now throw a cloth over the cage, which you lift quickly and briefly to remove the container. With any luck at all, the move from one cage to the other will function much more smoothly.

Now keep at a reasonable distance from the cage and watch the bird without approaching it. Speak to it softly and soothingly and do not make any sudden moves. Make sure everything is quiet and that there is enough light for the bird to see its surroundings. It is important at this initial stage not to change anything at all in or near the cage. Always approach the cage from the front and softly repeat the same sentences, preferably with the name of the bird in them. When you have to change the food or water, always repeat the same thing while performing the necessary tasks, and stay calm and unruffled even if the bird shrieks or startles you by fluttering unexpectedly.

How Should the Bird Sleep?

Leave a 15-watt bulb burning in the cockatiel's room for the first few nights. If noises from the street or in the house startle it, the light will keep it from panicking and fluttering wildly in the cage and hurting itself. Being able to see will reassure it that no danger is lurking in the immediate vicinity.

You have to decide for yourself whether or not you are going to drape a cloth over the cage at night. During the first few nights at least the bird should have the light from a weak bulb and the cage should not be covered. After a few days, the bulb can be replaced with the type of nightlight that is often used in children's bedrooms so that they will not be afraid of the dark. Once the bird has adjusted to its new home, it can sleep in a dark room. If, however, the room is used for hours after darkness falls or if a street light shines into it all night, it is better to protect the bird from the light and perhaps to dampen sounds. Ultimately it is best to let the bird decide how it would like to spend the night. You will be able to tell from its reaction whether it feels comfortable under the cloth or whether the cloth bothers it. If you do use a cloth, be sure to remove it early in the morning so that the bird has a 12-hour day if possible.

No matter how an acclimated bird spends its nights, it may happen occasionally that some unusual noise sends it into a panic. It will make a frantic attempt to flee and flutter around the cage wildly. If that happens, someone should go and look after the bird, turn the light on briefly, and calm it down.

Getting Your Cockatiel to Feel at Home

Rules for the First Few Days

Observe the following points during the first few days or weeks the bird spends in your home. Avoid anything that scares the bird as, for instance:

- loud noise, constant activity near it, and above all, slamming doors;
- any jolting of its cage;
- sudden movements in its vicinity;
- bright light in the evening (only dim light should reach the cage);
- direct exposure to the TV or loud sound from it;
- wearing very bright or very dark clothing, startling hats, curlers;
- disturbing its night's rest.

Something to remember at all times: If you do not want to risk losing the bird's confidence, never grab hold of it unless absolutely necessary. No bird likes to be grabbed. Its instincts tell it that this means mortal danger. (There are occasions when you do have to get hold of your bird, such as when it needs some medical treatment or when it has got itself into some desperate spot. Turn to p. 14 and 36 to find out how to do it properly.)

Getting Acquainted

If you spend some time during the first few days quietly going about your business near your cockatiel's cage, talk to it occasionally, and watch it, you will notice that it begins to relax in your presence, sometimes fluffs up its feathers and preens itself, and eats and drinks, though often darting a glance at you while doing so. This means that it has overcome its worst fears. Gradually it will get used to your doings in the cage and will begin to associate you with eating and drinking. Start in the first days sticking some parsley, lettuce leaves, and pieces of apples or carrots between the bars of the cage. If it is not introduced to these healthy foods at the beginning the bird may be reluctant to try them later.

Perhaps you will be able to tell which kinds of seeds it likes best. Then you can offer them to it through the bars one at a time, stuck lightly in the notched end of a twig. Tempt the bird closer and closer until one day it picks the treat from your fingertips. Once the bird no longer reacts with fear to your reaching into the cage to arrange something there, you should always offer it a special treat on the open palm of your hand when you have finished. Do not be startled, however, if the bird initially pecks at your hand. In part it is still fearful and wants to defend itself, and in part it is seeking to make contact. It is pecking, so to speak, to check if there will be a negative reaction. Do not jerk back your hand, and in general avoid sudden movements.

The day will come when the cockatiel will allow you to gently stroke its tummy with your

Figure 14 *Once a cockatiel has fully adjusted to its new surroundings it should always leave its cage by way of your hand. This way it will become familiar with your hand, and it will later choose your shoulder as a perch.*

Getting Your Cockatiel to Feel at Home

finger while it is sitting in its cage. Repeat this stroking every day, gradually increasing the pressure against the abdomen. At some point the bird will move from its perch to your finger while you are stroking it, and that will mark the beginning of it becoming hand tamed. But keep handling it very gently and avoid anything that might scare it.

The First Flight in the Room

Some experts recommend categorically that you wait about six weeks before allowing your bird to fly in the room. It is my feeling that you should not wait this long if your bird seems to feel comfortable in its new surroundings after a few days or in one or two weeks and no longer shies away from your hand. After all, a bird's well-being depends largely on it being allowed to fly enough. The need to fly disappears only if the bird is forced by pain to give up flying or if it is weak with age or very sick. Although tame cockatiels can get most places by climbing and like to march across the floor, flying is their natural mode of locomotion and is beneficial to their overall health. So the decision of when to let your cockatiel first fly free really depends on how quickly it feels at ease with you

One important question *before* you let the bird fly is, Do you have shades or blinds over your windows? A bird does not recognize the glass of a window as a barrier but thinks instead that the window leads to the outside and will bump into it, possibly breaking its neck. Therefore lower the shades about three quarters of the way before opening the cage (turn on the electric light if necessary for additional brightness in the room). Then you can lower the shade a little less every day until it is no longer necessary at all because the cockatiel has learned that the window forms part of the border of its flying area.

Also make sure all doors and windows are closed before you open the cage. Then let the bird do as it wishes. Perhaps it will take off immediately, but more likely it will first stare at this square of its cage that looks so changed. Then it may perch in the opening and peer out. Maybe it will climb on top of the cage to sit there for a while and contemplate the world from this new vantage point. Whatever it does, sooner or later the urge to fly will outweigh the shyness, and your cockatiel will take to its wings for the first time in your home.

Will it be able to land again back on top of its cage? Sometimes it will succeed, but often it will alight on some other spot because it is no longer used to the exertion of flying and needs to rest. Then it will sit anxiously in this unfamiliar spot. Give it time. If it cannot muster the courage to fly back after 10 or 15 minutes, you might hold the cage near it in such a way that it can enter it easily. If the bird is sitting in an inaccessible place, let it sit—overnight if necessary—until it flies back on its own. If you approach it with brooms, waving cloths, or other sinister objects in your effort to rouse it from its perch, it will come away with the indelible impression that people are its worst enemies.

From now on, open the cage at the same time every day. The desire to fly is irresistible, and your cockatiel will have less and less trouble returning to its cage without help. When the flying session has proceeded smoothly several times, start letting the bird out only on your hand. Place your finger or the back of your hand in front of it, and lift it out of the cage. The reason for this is that it will get more used to your hand and will learn to think of it as being helpful.

When your cockatiel is totally at ease with you, it will alight on your shoulder for the first time. Walk up and down with it there, talking to it or whistling or singing some tune to it. It will stay on your shoulder longer each time and gradually regard it as the ideal landing site.

Getting Your Cockatiel to Feel at Home

Everyday Life with Your Bird

From now on you should leave it up to the cockatiel whether it spends its days in the cage or on the climbing tree or in some other favorite place in the room. If you see to it that it gets all its food in the cage, it will always return there willingly to rest. Catch these moments to close the cage door if you have to leave the room for some time. When your cockatiel has become totally trusting it will also come to your hand without much resistance when you want to return it to its cage.

You will have no trouble telling what your bird likes and dislikes, what the most tempting objects are for working on with the beak, and what else arouses its curiosity. Bird-proof the room by removing everything that could cause injury or be otherwise harmful to your bird (pp. 33–34) and what you want to protect from it. Unfortunately there is no effective way to prevent the gradual shredding of wallpaper and the gnawing of protruding edges and corners. The best you can do is to provide a climbing tree where it will spend most of its time, especially if it often finds fresh branches there. Once it has gotten used to thinking of its cage and its tree as its very own territory and you are thoroughly familiar with its habits, you can leave it in the bird-proofed room for a reasonable time without locking it in its cage. Just make sure no window or door is opened even a crack.

The more unconfined a bird feels, the more relaxed it will stay if it has to be by itself part of the time. It will then be particularly intent on being close to the people it knows when they are there, taking part in their activities and maintaining voice contact. Your cockatiel may land on your desk where you are working, checking everything to see what it is good for and starting to work with it. The culmination of its activities will be the deliberately engineered and noisy fall of moveable objects. My cockatiel Koko, for instance, always worked very hard to move the box with my writing implements across the desk until the whole thing crashed to the floor.

After a while you should pay closer attention to what your cockatiel is muttering to itself. Perhaps you will recognize some words it has heard a lot. Repeat these often with deliberately clear enunciation. It is best if the person the bird knows best does this. Also keep in mind that the bird learns best when there is not much else going on in the room and when the bird itself is not occupied with something else.

This is also the time to whistle simple, short melodies to it over and over. Cockatiels have a special talent for whistling and like to imitate tunes. But all birds with a gift for vocal mimicry repeat not only words and melodies you teach them deliberately. They will also soon reproduce phrases of greeting and farewell, the "Hello" they hear you say on the telephone, and exclamations they hear a lot. Your cockatiel will be most enthusiastic about repeating anything that makes a big impression on it, anything that is repeated over and over, and especially anything that is related to your display of affection for it. The old saying that you first have to loosen a bird's tongue by force before it learns to speak is nonsense and cruelty to animals.

Plate 3 Upper left: *Curtains provide a much appreciated opportunity for climbing.*
Upper right: *A male cockatiel in his showing-off posture.*
Below: *Cockatiels preening themselves.*

Good Care and Proper Nutrition

Daily Care

Looking after a cockatiel is not complicated, but whatever care it needs must be provided conscientiously and regularly.

• *Daily*

Empty food and water dishes, rinse the with very hot water, dry them well, and fill them again. Remove droppings and seed husks from the sand in the cage and in the tub with the climbing tree. Use a slotted spoon that is reserved for this. Dirty branches and perches can be taken out and brushed under hot water; branches that cannot be moved should be brushed off repeatedly with warm water in the cage or on the tree. (Old toothbrushes work well for this.)

• *At least twice a week*

Change the sand. Rinse the bottom tray of the cage well under warm water and dry before filling in the new sand.

• *Once a week*

Wash out the base of the cage on which the metal top stands. Toys both inside and outside the cage also have to be washed in hot water once a week or more often if necessary.

• *Once a month*

Place the metal part of the cage in the bathtub or some other big tub and let it soak in warm water. Then squirt clear water over all parts and dry them with a soft cloth. Spray perches or branches and their mountings with a mite spray.

If your bird has taken a bath in its bathhouse (use rainwater), the house has to be rinsed in hot water, dried, and stored until the next bath.

Important: Plain water is best for cleaning the cage and everything else your bird uses. Cleansers and rinses are harmful or even fatal to all birds.

Spreading sand on the bottom of the cage is done not only for hygienic reasons but also for the sake of the bird's health. The bird will eat a little bit of sand every day as an aid to digestion. Bird sand also contains calcium and other minerals. If you cover the cage floor with sandpaper sheets that pet stores sell (in different sizes), the cockatiel will be able to peck a few grains of sand off it, but it will not get the mineral supplements through this that are so important to its health.

Here is a compromise solution: If you favor this sandpaper because it does not cause dust, always have a little dish with bird sand in the cage.

The Basic Food

Half-ripe seeds, the most important source of nourishment for wild cockatiels, are available for only part of the year after the rainy seasons in their native habitat in Australia. The rest of the time the birds live primarily on fully ripened, dry seeds of various grasses and wild grains. Commercial birdseed mixtures you can buy include various kinds of millet, canary or white seed, oats, black and white sunflower seeds, hemp seed, and wheat kernels. This mixture contains all the carbohydrates, fats, proteins, and minerals and vitamins a bird needs. The amount of minerals and vitamins depends on the time of harvest, the conditions of storage, and the length of shelf life of the seeds. As a general rule one can assume that seeds maintain their nutritional value with some gradual decrease for about one year and are useable for another year.

It is not advisable to buy birdseed that claims to be designed for both cockatiels and parrots because a cockatiel will refuse to eat a significant portion of this food, such as nuts with hard shells, corn, and acorns.

In time you will learn what kinds of seeds your bird likes especially. Offer it some of them from your hand occasionally to win its affections and to give it a treat. But do not buy this kind of seed separately and mix it in with the bird's daily fare. Its food would then be too one-sided and possibly too high in fats, because cockatiels have a special weakness for sunflower and hemp seeds, both of which are high in fats.

You can find birdseed mixtures for cockatiels at

29

seed stores, pet shops, and the supermarket. Always check the date of packing, which is usually stamped on the bottom of the package. If you want to be sure your cockatiel is getting all the vitamins it needs, buy only packages that are less than one year old. And observe the following:

• Whatever mixture you buy, check on the quality by trying to sprout some of the seeds. It is fair to say that seeds that germinate within 48 hours have much more nutritional value than ones that do not.

• Any mixture of seeds represents only the basic staple of a bird's food. Your cockatiel also needs sprouted seeds, greens, fruit, and fresh branches.

Sprouted Seeds

When viable seeds absorb water, a chemical reaction is set in motion that results in their sprouting. In the process, vitamins, minerals, and trace elements are released, which add to the nutritive value of the seeds.

Soak about one tablespoonful of the seed mixture per day in some water. The water should cover the seeds by about 1 inch (2 cm). Let them sit for 24 hours, then rinse them well with lukewarm water and offer them to the cockatiel in a flat dish. Loosely covered – not airtight – the seeds will stay fresh for 24 to 48 hours. If you feed them after 24 hours, the seeds will be swollen and after 48 hours they have sprouted. Rinse the seeds once more thoroughly and let the water drip out before feeding.

Important: Swollen and sprouted seeds spoil quickly. Give this valuable food in a special dish in the morning and remove what is left over around noon. This way you keep the bird from eating deteriorating food that might make it sick. In time you will know just how much your bird will eat. You will also notice that for a while it will avidly consume all the sprouted food you

give it and then it may ignore it for days or weeks. Stop feeding it sprouted seeds temporarily when you notice that it has lost interest in them.

Supplementary Foods

In addition to its basic food, your cockatiel needs some fresh greens and/or fruit every day. The sooner you get it accustomed to this, the more of this kind of food it will consume. Always try to offer it two different kinds of fresh food. If it gets only parsley or only apples and happens not to have a taste for them at the time, it will not touch them. But if it has a choice, it may accept one of the alternatives.

Important: Do not feed anything that comes straight from the refrigerator and is still cold. Nor can you feed it old, withered, let alone decaying fruit or greens. Everything has to be washed in lukewarm water and dried with a towel before being fed.

Beneficial greens: parsley, spinach, beet greens, lettuce, endive, corn salad, carrot tops, chickweed, dandelion greens, and, in the spring when they have buds, fresh branches from fruit trees, willows, or hazelnut bushes. If you pick the greens yourself, stay away from fields and bushes along highways because the sediment of poisonous exhaust fumes cannot be washed off completely and can be fatal to birds.

Beneficial fruits and root vegetables: apples, pears, strawberries, grapes, kiwi fruit, cherries, rowanberries, washed and scraped carrots, and peeled kohlrabi. If your cockatiel shows no interest in pieces of carrot or kohlrabi, try these vegetables in grated form.

The Importance of Vitamins

Everyone knows that parsley, for instance, is full of vitamin A. But there are few vitamins left in

Good Care and Proper Nutrition

parsley that is old and wilted, kept artificially fresh, or grown in poor soil. This is true for all plants that are sources of vitamins. But vitamins are crucial, and the smaller the organism the more it will react to poor food. Many serious disorders in birds are the consequence of chronic insufficiency of vitamins. That is why I urge you to add vitamins to your cockatiel's drinking water even if you do supply it with varied fresh foods. I use multivitamins that I buy at the pet store for my birds and add a few drops of liquid vitamins or the tip of a knife's worth of the powdered form to their drinking water every day. The pet food industry offers many vitamin combinations that can be given in the drinking water or sprinkled over the birdseed.

Calcium and Phosphorus

The foods we have discussed thus far contain very little of these minerals. To make up for this, you should give your bird a mineral stone on which to nibble and sharpen its beak. These stones are available at pet stores. Always keep one in reserve because sometimes a bird does not touch the stone for weeks and then suddenly gnaws on it constantly until it disintegrates. When you buy the stone, make sure it says on the package something like: "Mineral stone containing all elements necessary for strengthening the skeleton and forming feathers of birds." Instead of an artificial stone like this you can also buy cuttlebone or sepia, which are the calcium-rich internal shells of cuttlefish. Some cockatiels prefer sepia to mineral stones. The bird sand in the bottom of the cage also contains calcium.
Giving pet birds crushed eggshells — whether from raw or cooked eggs — as a source of calcium is not advisable because, first of all, these shells can be carriers of salmonella and other bacteria and, secondly, calcium is the only useful mineral they contain.

Those Little Extras

In addition to the foods mentioned, cockatiels should get some spray millet every day. This healthy treat is even recommended as the sole food during an illness. Pet stores also sell "cookies" in the shape of rings, hearts, and sticks. These are made up of a normal birdseed mixture that is held together with some honey or sweet syrup. Since it takes some work with the beak to get the grains and seeds out, birds usually like these special treats. Cockatiels also like to nibble on zwieback and special bird wafers available at pet stores. And about twice a week you should serve your bird a special treat in the form of a quarter of a hard-boiled and finely chopped egg.

Rules about Feeding

Birds have an especially high rate of metabolism and therefore need to eat more frequently than mammals, for instance. You should give your bird its food and water at the same time every day. There is no need to carefully measure the amount of food as long as the mixture of seeds is well balanced. There is only one problem: Cockatiels cleverly shell the seeds with their beaks and let the empty husks drop into the dish. After a few snacks the birds can no longer find the seeds toward the bottom of the dish and you have to remove the layer of empty husks on top. To prevent possible disaster in case you forget to do this, offer the seeds in several flat dishes. Remove the husks once or twice a day with a small spoon, or remove them by blowing over the seed. Remember that you may unexpectedly be delayed or prevented from coming home some day. Always put enough food in the cage to last for a couple of days in an emergency. This is another good reason to hang some spray millet in the cage. Also, old drinking water is better than none at all if for some reason you are prevented from doing the chores for your

31

Good Care and Proper Nutrition

Figure 15 *Unlike large parrots, cockatiels do not use their feet to place food in their bills but step on the food instead to keep it in place while they nibble on it.*

bird. As a general rule you need not worry about overfeeding your bird. A healthy bird that gets enough attention from people and has things to keep busy with is in no danger of growing obese. But be careful not to let your cockatiel sample your food. Sausage, cheese, butter, milk, coffee, beer, and spices are harmful for it. They can cause diarrhea or permanent molt and even fatty degeneration of the liver, which may be fatal.

If your cockatiel is in the same room where you eat and has an inclination to taste your food, you should lock it in its cage at mealtimes. But if you are sitting around in the evening having a good time together munching on some nuts or crackers, you can allow your pet to nibble on a peanut or a cracker without worry.

Drinking Water

Only in an extreme emergency can a cockatiel be left without water for a whole day. Observation in Australia has shown that these birds frequent watering spots three to four times a day to drink or bathe or both. Pet cockatiels that are generally kept in heated and therefore dry rooms need fresh drinking water at all times. The water should contain as little chlorine as possible. If your tap water is strongly chlorinated, you should give your cockatiel rain or spring water. The latter is sold at pet and grocery stores, and is an especially pure and salutary drinking water. There is no need to give your cockatiel boiled water or herb teas unless the veterinarian recommends it for treating an intestinal disorder. But the normal drinking water should never be cold and should be given fresh every day; in the summer or if the water gets dirty, it should be replaced two or three times a day. I have already mentioned that the drinking dish should not be covered.

Figure 16 *Automatic water dispensers are especially useful when the water supply has to last while you are gone for several hours or even a day or two.*

Hazards In Your Home

Your cockatiel is exposed to all kinds of dangers in your home even if it is healthy, tame, well nourished, and cheerful. I will mention the most frequent causes of accidents and injuries so that you can take precautions against them.

The Greatest Danger: Flying Away

Most birds that fly away from home and are not fortunate enough to be picked up by other people perish miserably. There are many ways for a cockatiel to escape:
- open doors and windows;
- a cage door that is not fastened properly;
- cage bars that are set too widely so that the bird can slip through them.

Many people with cockatiels think that venetian blinds in front of an open window will keep their bird from flying away. But cockatiels like to climb up on the slats, slip through a tiny opening, climb down the other side – and they are gone. This is why I had a heavy screen made for one window in the room where I keep my bird. The screen is made of a light wooden frame covered with ½ inch (1 cm) wire mesh and fits into the window frame. This allows me to open the window for airing the room or to leave it open without worrying that the bird will take off when I happen to have my back toward it.

Even the tamest cockatiel that is used to staying by its person's side with the window open, on the balcony, or while taking out the garbage, or on the way to the car, can after years without incident be scared by a loud noise, flutter up in panic, and fly out of sight. Then it may not know how to get back, and the greater its fear of this unfamiliar world, the faster it will fly.

Out of 100 carefully kept cockatiels about 60 will escape "by mistake." This shows that flying away is by far the greatest danger. To try to minimize other hazards, study the following list of dangers.

Catalog of Everyday Dangers

Drafts when airing the room: Cockatiels are very sensitive to drafts and easily catch pneumonia or inflammation of the crop.

Direct sun, overheated rooms: If the bird cannot move into the shade, it may suffer a heatstroke.

Sudden changes in temperature: The acceptable range of temperatures is from 75°F down to 41°F (24–5°C). Birds have to get acclimated gradually to different temperatures.

Cracks between furniture and walls: Slipping down and getting stuck.

Bookshelves: Climbing behind the books and not being able to get out without help.

Drawers and closets: The curious bird will want to investigate what is in them. If you lock it in inadvertently, it may suffocate or starve.

Kitchen: Steam and vapors; suffocating; heat from stoves and subsequent airing can lead to colds.

Hot pots and dishes with hot food: Burns and drowning.

Hot stove top: Burns, possibly fatal.

Traces of cleansers and chemicals: Poisoning.

Tilted casement window: Escaping.

Open toilet bowl: Sliding in and drowning.

Figure 17   *A kitchen is full of hazards.*

33

Hazards In Your Home

Bathtubs, sinks, and tubs with water: Drowning. Soapsuds on the water's surface look like a landing area.

Window glass, glass walls: Flying against the glass, sustaining concussion or breaking skull or neck.

Doors: Getting caught in them and squashed.

Stoves and electrical devices: Burns, possibly fatal.

Electrical wires and outlets: Electric shock if chewed on.

Candlelight: Dangerous for a free-flying bird. Burns or catching on fire.

Empty vases and other ornamental containers: Sliding in and being unable to climb out again. Suffocating, starving, heart attack. (Fill the containers with sand or paper.)

Beer mugs and tall glasses: Sliding in, drowning, suffocating. (Cover and store upside down.)

*Knitted and crocheted items:*Getting toes caught and hanging upside down.

Yarn, thread, chains: Getting entangled and strangling.

Hard floors: Birds with limited flying abilities may land too hard and break legs or bruise chest.

Improper spacing of wires or bars in cages and aviaries: Sticking the head through and strangling or sustaining other injuries.

Thin, sharp wire: Cuts on toes and head.

Perches that are too thin: Overgrowth of claws and cartilaginous growths.

Sharp objects, ends of wire, nails, splinters: Puncture wounds and other injuries.

Human feet: Being stepped on.

Chairs and sofas: Being sat on and crushed.

Poisons: Deadly poisons are lead, verdigris, rust, protective coatings on cooking utensils, cleaning agents, mercury. Also harmful are lead tips of pencils, writing tips of ballpoint and felt-tip pens, alcohol, coffee, strong spices.

Plant insecticides: Anything that claims to kill insects is bad for birds. Never spray the plants in the "bird room," and do not bring in plants that have been sprayed.

Poisonous plants: Yew, narcissus, primrose, oleander.

Cacti: The spines can cause serious eye and skin injuries.

Nicotine: Smoke-filled air is bad. Nicotine is deadly.

Mites and other pests: Disinfect cage, toys, and your bird's favorite spots, but never dust or spray the bird. This could lead to suffocation or poisoning. If the bird has parasites, take it to the veterinarian.

Food intended for humans: Generally bad for birds.

If Your Cockatiel Gets Sick

Outward Signs

A cockatiel that is not feeling well shows this in its behavior (Figure 18). It sits on its perch apathetically with the head turned and the beak tucked in the feathers on the back. It will follow with a tired glance what happens in its immediate vicinity. The feathers are fluffed up, and the bird rests on both legs instead of on one as it normally does. To be sure, sitting or sleeping on both legs is in itself no indication of illness. Some cockatiels sleep standing on both legs all the time. But illness will manifest itself in other symptoms as well: The bird will eat much less frequently than usual and then only a little bit. If it is in really bad shape, it may squat weakly on the bottom of its cage. If it stays on its favorite branch, it will no longer sit upright as usual, but hold its body almost horizontally with a slight downward droop of the tail. If it is in pain, it will periodically angle the wings sideways from the body with a slight tremble and bite into the air. Often, the breathing of sick birds is labored.

Examine the bird's droppings with special care. If they are slimy, runny, or watery, this is cause for alarm. An occasional watery dropping when the cockatiel does not look sick can simply be a sign of harmless indigestion. Some cockatiels also produce a watery dropping soon after taking a bath or if they have been frightened.

Another sign of danger is if the bird is trying to cough up phlegm from the crop or throat. In such a case, the bird keeps gagging and shaking its head, trying to get rid of the slime. But again, do not be frightened if a healthy bird opens its beak wide several times in succession while pulling itself up to its full height in a way that suggests yawning and stretching. This is in fact a healthy bird's way of trying to overcome a shortage of oxygen. And if the bird makes noises that sound like sneezes, this occurs because it cannot blow its nose in a tissue.

Medical and First Aid Supplies for Your Bird

Anyone keeping a bird should have a few items and utensils for first aid on hand: blunt tweezers, a pipette, scissors with rounded points, some iodine, plain and styptic cotton, charcoal, and some narrow bandages.

Important: If you do not have one already, buy an infrared lamp (Figure 19).

A sick bird should have a cage to itself. If you have a pair of birds, leave the sick bird where it is and move the other one into a second cage, if necessary in a different room. The room with the sick bird in it has to be warm and quiet and without glaring lights. Shine the infrared light on the bird. It radiates not only heat but also penetrates under the skin and stimulates blood circulation and metabolism. The blood vessels expand so that the harmful substances can be eliminated more quickly. The rays also activate the production of antibodies. The lamp should be about 16 inches (40 cm) from the cage. Check the temperature carefully and make sure it does not rise above 95°F (35°C). Turn the lamp on three to four times daily for half an hour to an hour. If a bird looks

Figure 18 *If your bird's feathers are puffed up and it sits on the bottom of its cage, hardly eating, it is seriously sick and should be taken to the veterinarian.*

35

very sick, the infrared light can be left on day and night if necessary. The even heat from it is beneficial. But make sure the bird can get away from the rays in its cage in case it gets too warm. The light from the lamp should therefore shine on only half of the cage.

Important: When the infrared lamp is turned off, the temperature in the cage should not drop rapidly. Try to maintain it at about 86°F (30°C) by shining an electric bulb behind a cloth into the cage.

If the bird has come down with a respiratory ailment — it coughs up phlegm, has a discharge from the nose, and is breathing with a light rattle — you have to make sure the air humidity stays high enough while you shine a lamp into the cage. A good way to do this is to place a bowl with hot water near the cage. Make sure the cage is shut so the bird will not get close to the water.

These first measures are not enough if the symptoms persist. If the bird still looks sick after several hours, take it to the veterinarian or ask the veterinarian to make a house call. If you have to transport the bird, make sure its surrounding temperature stays the same, i.e., drive with the heat turned on in the car. Drape a warm cover loosely over the cage.

Figure 19 *Infrared rays help activate the production of antibodies.*

Advice on handling the bird: If you have to get hold of the bird, reach for it in the right way: Place your right hand against its breast, and reach down from above with the left hand over the bird's head. This way the bird's head rests between your thumb and forefinger, and the other fingers are wrapped around the belly. This lets you look the bird over belly up and leaves your right hand to perform whatever measures are necessary. Never catch a bird in the air. It is too easy to injure a wing or shoulder joint this way. If the bird is not tame enough to let itself be caught during the day, wait until evening and get hold of it when it gets dark.

Diseases Affecting Cockatiels and What You Can Do about Them

Molt (not a disease)

Symptoms: More or less serious loss of feathers, in older birds sometimes to the extent of making them unable to fly. Lasts two to three weeks. Happens two to three times a year in captivity, without respect to external factors.

Cause: Renewal of plumage.

Treatment: Feed diet rich in minerals and vitamins, i.e., sprouted seeds, greens, fruit, calcium; keep bird evenly warm and quiet. Older birds can get weak and sickly at these times and should then be exposed to infrared light up to three times a day.

Permanent Molt

Symptoms: Loss of feathers extending over months and causing bald spots. May be accompanied by (a) a great restlessness and the bird's grooming itself compulsively, (b) diarrhea with yellowish to brownish droppings, (c) malformed new feathers, (d) obesity.

Causes: (a) Presence of parasites, especially of red bird mites (p. 38). (b) Deficiencies in vitamins and minerals can cause metabolic disorders that

36

cause increased itching. Frequently, old, rancid seeds are the cause. Yellowish to brownish droppings indicate liver ailments. In this case, the veterinarian should prescribe a liver medication. (c) Inadequate diet over a long period of time. (d) Cockatiels that are overfed and do not get enough exercise can develop obesity that is often accompanied by violent itching. The remedy here is to limit the birdseed to two tablespoons a day of the best kinds of seeds, given preferably in two feedings. The mixture should contain no hemp and very little sunflower seed because these seeds contain about 50% fat. Millet and seed "cookies" should also be eliminated, and the bird kept in a cool room.

First measures: Plenty of vitamins and minerals in the food, i.e., sprouted seeds, greens, fruit, calcium; (even) heat and quiet.

Treatment: The veterinarian can administer more specialized treatment.

Feather Pulling

Symptoms: The bird pulls out its feathers (Figure 20) for no apparent reason, creating blood-encrusted places or even totally bare parts of the body.

Figure 20 *Feather plucking occurs among cockatiels, too.*

Possible causes: Veterinarians disagree about the causes. Psychic disorders resulting from boredom, loneliness, or grief over losing a partner (including human partners) have been blamed, as have dry air (central heating), deficiencies caused by metabolic disorders, itching because of obesity, chronic inflammation of the skin, and latent poisoning due to consumption of spray millet treated with insecticides.

First measures: Added protein in the diet in the form of ant pupae, hard-boiled egg yolk, or cottage cheese; fresh branches to chew on; providing a climbing tree; spending more time with the bird; getting it a partner.

Treatment: Consult a veterinarian who specializes in parrots.

Lumps under the Skin

Symptoms: (a) Small swellings, (b) fat deposits underneath the skin, (c) air pockets, (d) cysts in the feather follicles.

Possible causes and first measures: (a) Nonmalignant tumors in the fatty tissues (lipoma) can be surgically removed under anesthesia. (b) Fat deposits differ from tumors in showing a yellowish color through the skin; tumors are almost always accompanied by a thickening of the skin (see *Permanent molt*). (c) Tears in air sacs beneath the skin can result in air accumulations that cause the skin to bulge out like little balloons. The air sacs are connected with the lungs and aerate the hollow wing bones. Some of them extend to just beneath the skin; and if such a sac is injured in a collision or fall, the air leaks out of it, puffing out the skin. Only a veterinarian should prick such an air pocket to let the air escape. After this, the bird should stay in its cage for at least a week, so that the tear can heal completely. (d) Cysts about the size of the head of a pin form in the feather follicles if the new feathers cannot penetrate through the skin. If you notice your bird constantly probing such a spot in its plumage, take it to the veterinarian.

If Your Cockatiel Gets Sick

Injuries of the Skin

Symptoms: Bloody feathers, blood on the perches.

Possible causes: Tears or cuts caused by sharp objects, by torn or deteriorating cage grating, by injured claws, or by bites from other birds.

First measures: Apply styptic cotton only in case of serious bleeding; leave minor wounds alone.

Treatment: In cases of strong bleeding due to injured blood vessels – especially on the head and crop – call the veterinarian immediately.

Parasites

Symptoms: The birds keep scratching, peck at the feathers and skin, and are often very restless, especially at night.

Possible causes: Red bird mites, feather mites, or lice.

First measures: Feather mites and lice can be spotted with the naked eye. Red mites bother birds at night by sucking their blood. During the day they retreat to dark, hidden spots. If you cannot detect either lice or feather mites in the plumage of your bird, it most likely is suffering from red mites. Drape a white cloth over the cage overnight, and the next morning you will find tiny red and black moving dots on it. The first step is to disinfect and treat with mite spray all wooden parts of the cage and possibly the climbing tree and other objects in the bird's vicinity as well. Repeat this four to five times at two- to three-week intervals until you are sure all traces of mites have been destroyed. If infested with feather mites or lice, the bird itself has to be treated with a powder recommended by the veterinarian.

When you treat the cage and other surroundings of the bird with the mite spray, the bird has to be moved to another room for the duration of the spraying.

Caution: Never use the spray on the bird! Even if you cover its head carefully, the bird may inhale the spray with the severe consequences of extreme difficulty in breathing or edema of the lungs. The spray also irritates the eyes and causes inflammations, and it penetrates the very thin skin of birds, is absorbed by the body, and leads to symptoms of poisoning. Any kind of spray can cause poisoning, and you should therefore always use powders for treating birds.

Mycosis of the Beak

Symptoms: Sponge-like, whitish gray growths on the beak, the ceres, near the eyes, and sometimes on the legs. Starting out as a barely visible grayish layer, the mange can develop into horn-like growths.

Possible cause: Mange mites.

First measures: None.

Treatment: If the legs are affected, immediately remove the band because the legs can thicken rapidly causing the band to constrict the leg. Take the bird to the veterinarian and follow the treatment prescribed by him.

Overgrown Claws

Symptoms: Frequent catching of the toes, overly long nails, sometimes curling in spiral shape.

Possible causes: Perches that are too thin and too smooth; not enough opportunity to move around on natural branches.

Figure 21 *When you trim your cockatiel's toenails, hold the foot up against the light so that you can see clearly how far the blood vessels reach into the nail.*

If Your Cockatiel Gets Sick

First measures: Supply natural branches of varying thickness and rough stones. Trim claws: Hold the bird in your left hand as described earlier and hold the toes up against a bright light so that the dark blood vessels in the claws are easily visible. Cut the claws carefully just short of the blood vessels (see Figure 21). If there should be some bleeding, press some styptic cotton against the toes. By the time the cotton falls off, the blood has usually stopped running. If you do not feel confident about trying this yourself, let the veterinarian do it.

Figure 22 *This is how you should hold your cockatiel when you trim its claws. Hold the bird's head and bill firmly between your thumb and forefinger so that it cannot bite you.*

Overgrown Beak

Symptoms: The upper, or occasionally the lower, mandible grows too much, bending sideways and curling down (or up) so that the bird can no longer eat.

Possible causes: Improper diet and not enough wearing down of the bill. Many ornithologists think that in most cases there is a congenital factor involved.

First measures: None.

Treatment: The veterinarian may have to trim the bill periodically.

Constipation

Symptoms: The bird has to strain to produce droppings and wags its tail end back and forth in the process.

Possible causes: Improper diet; obesity; in very old birds, sluggishness of the intestines; pelvic growths, which are luckily rare in cockatiels.

First measures: Feed a lot of fruit, greens, and especially sprouted seeds; let the bird move freely as much as possible.

Caution: Female cockatiels exhibit similar symptoms when suffering from egg binding.

Treatment: If the bird fails to produce any droppings after about four hours of trying, take it to the veterinarian.

Diarrhea

If your cockatiel's stool is occasionally runny, or even watery, this is not necessarily a pathological sign. You cannot give a healthy bird too much fruit and greens, and these foods often result in soft to watery droppings, caused by the acidity of fruit. This is perfectly harmless as long as the bird behaves normally and does not look sick. Some owners of birds permanently eliminate fruit and greens from their cockatiels' diet because they mistakenly believe that the thin consistency of the stool is necessarily a sign of illness.

Symptoms of abnormal diarrhea: Watery or runny and often discolored droppings; dirty feathers around the cloaca; noticeably apathetic or otherwise changed behavior.

Possible causes: Colds from drafts or sudden changes of temperature; drinking or bath water that is too cold; cold or spoiled food; decaying fruit or greens; food that is too salty or spicy; nibbling on indigestible or poisonous substances such as lead paint, or some house plants; inflammation of the stomach, intestines, or kidneys;

39

infections; parasite infestations; metabolic disorders; or psychological disturbances.

First measures: Wash the dirty feathers with lukewarm water and let dry well. Use of an infrared lamp is recommended. Isolate sick bird from others.

Important: No fresh food; sprinkle charcoal on the seeds; if diarrhea persists, toast seeds slightly, and give boiled water or lukewarm camomile tea. In cases of bad diarrhea you can also feed the bird zwieback or dry bread dunked into camomile tea since the bird may need extra liquid, having lost fluids through the diarrhea. Provide even warmth and quiet.

Treatment: If the diarrhea lasts more than 12 hours and the bird's behavior is changed, showing weakness and other symptoms, you have to assume that there is some serious disease. Never just get a prescription for an all-purpose antibiotic but insist on an analysis of the stool to determine the exact cause of the disorder.

Fractures

Symptoms: Fractures of the tarsus or toes are visible, but those of the drumstick and thigh are not because these parts of the leg are buried in the body. But restrictions of movement will indicate fractures. Fractures of the wings can also be seen.

Possible causes: Falls, collisions, getting caught in something.

First measures: Place a bird with a broken leg in a separate cage with a perch where it can rest for two weeks. Food and water dishes should be hung to the sides of the cage at perch level so the bird can reach them easily. The bird should sit on the perch so that the broken leg can hang down without any weight being put on it. Broken wings should be bandaged properly by a veterinarian.

Clogged Oil Gland

Symptoms: Swelling of the oil or preen gland at the base of the tail; the bird pecks at it and causes it to become red and inflamed.

Possible causes: Clogged duct or tumor on the gland.

First measures: None.

Treatment: Consult the veterinarian.

Egg Binding

Symptoms: The female pushes as though she were constipated. Her lower belly is rounded, the feathers around the cloaca stand out lightly, and the ceres are light and smooth. If the egg cannot be passed, the female becomes weak, raises her plumage, whips her tail up and down strongly, keeps her eyes closed, and is reduced to squatting on the bottom of the cage.

Possible causes: General weakness; temperatures that are too cool; female is laying her first egg, or the egg has formed no calcium shell.

First measures: Treat with infrared light and warm steam.

Treatment: If the egg is not laid within one or two hours after the warmth treatment is started, call the veterinarian.

Breathing Difficulties

Symptoms: Weakness, trembling, labored breathing, squeaking or whistling sounds of breathing. The bird may hold onto the wire of the cage with the bill and stretch its neck in an attempt to get more air.

Possible causes: Heart weakness causing edema of the lungs; circulatory problems; infection of the air passages; colds caused by temperature changes or drafts; pneumonia.

First measures: None.

Treatment: Visit the veterinarian as soon as possible; make sure the temperature stays even on the way.

Crop Inflammation

Symptoms: Vomiting; sneezing; coughing; shaking of the head often accompanied by discharge of sour or bad smelling phlegm, gummed

If Your Cockatiel Gets Sick

nostrils; sticky feathers on the head; labored breathing.

Possible causes: Colds, infections, food that does not agree.

First measures: Wash dirty feathers with lukewarm water and dab thoroughly dry; exposure to infrared light essential; feed lukewarm camomile tea.

Treatment: If the condition does not improve within 24 hours, see the veterinarian; make sure the temperature stays even on the way.

Concussion

Symptoms: Sudden total paralysis or loss of consciousness.

Possible causes: A bad fall or collision with a window.

First measures: Keep a dazed bird quiet in a darkened cage for at least 24 hours. Lay an unconscious bird comfortably in a dark place with the head slightly higher than the body. If the bird is conscious, provide even warmth but do not use infrared lamp.

Treatment: Take the bird to the veterinarian as soon as possible; make sure the temperature stays even on the way and avoid all jolting.

Paralyzed Limbs

Symptoms: Slight dragging of one leg or gradually increasing restriction of movements.

Possible causes: Vitamin deficiencies – especially B vitamins – and, in egg-laying females, lack of calcium; sprained joints; pulled nerves; leg band that has grown into the leg.

First measures: Add vitamins to drinking water and feed fruit and greens; provide warmth but not infrared light.

Treatment: No matter what you think the cause may be, let the veterinarian have a look as soon as possible.

Cramps

Symptoms: The first sign usually is weakness of the legs; later, disturbed equilibrium, reeling on the ground, sitting mostly on the stomach; stereotypical head movements. In extreme cases, the head is bent convulsively to the stomach or to the back.

Possible causes: Lack of vitamins B or E and, in egg-laying females, of calcium; epilepsy; consequence of a concussion; lead poisoning; poisoning through inhaling solvents.

First measures: Even warmth, absolute quiet, indirect light, no infrared lamp.

Treatment: Call the veterinarian immediately.

Psittacosis ("Parrot Fever")

Symptoms: Apathy, diarrhea, head cold, conjunctivitis, emaciation, excessive drowsiness. When transmitted to human beings, the disease manifests symptoms similar to those of pneumonia and requires immediate treatment!

Possible causes: Microorganisms that can be combatted with antibiotics. Poorly kept birds that lack resistance are prone to psittacosis. The pathogens are eliminated with the stool, stick to the sand and feather dust, are circulated through the air by the fluttering birds, and get inhaled by the caged birds or by people. Older and sickly people and children are especially likely to get infected. Parrots and parrotlike birds are not the only carriers of the disease; native birds that show no symptoms may spread the disease without catching it themselves. Psittacosis, or ornithosis, as it is also called, has to be reported. Remember that dead birds must be burned.

First measures: None.

Treatment: Consult the veterinarian immediately.

While the Bird Is Healthy

Do not let this list of possible diseases alarm you. Generally, cockatiels are healthy and often live up to 15 or 20 years. Observe your healthy

bird minutely so that you will be able to tell immediately if something is wrong. Quiet, warmth,
loving care, and proper diet usually clear up
minor problems. Consult the veterinarian
promptly if your first measures fail to produce
results. The right treatment administered quickly
may spell the difference between life and death.
While the bird is healthy, try to find a veterinarian
who specializes in birds, or preferably parrots, or
who is at least experienced in treating birds.

Destroying a Sick Bird

The only defensible way to get rid of a sick pet,
if there is some urgent reason for it, is to have a
veterinarian put it to sleep.

What to Do with Your Bird When . . .

Often the pleasure of planning a vacation is spoiled by the question, What will happen to the cockatiel?

The best solution for the bird is if it can stay in its familiar surroundings. If you have a pair of birds, you can dismiss the worry that the birds will be lonely and mourn in your absence. It is perfectly adequate to have someone reliable come in once a day, preferably in the morning, to supply them with plenty of food and air the room. But a single cockatiel should not be left alone for weeks on end. Ideally one member of the family should stay behind and keep the bird company at least a few hours a day. If this is not feasible, take the bird to a friend's or relative's house, where it will get regular care. The first time it may react with fear to the new surroundings, but on a second occasion it may already recognize the place. Take along a sufficient amount of the birdseed the cockatiel is used to, as well as sand, the bathhouse, toys, and a list of instructions including special habits of the bird, its favorite supplementary foods and how much of them it should get every day, and whether and how often it likes to take baths. Be sure to draw the bird sitter's attention to possible dangers and causes of accidents (pp. 33–34).

If you cannot find anyone to look after your bird, it is possible to leave it alone in the apartment for two or three days. In this case, leave plenty of birdseed in several flat dishes because the bird will be unable to find the seeds under a thick layer of empty husks. You can also use an automatic feeder if you have tried it out before and if it functions reliably. Leave plenty of spray millet, too. Supply water in an automatic waterer the bird has previously gotten used to. But I consider it completely unfeasible to leave a bird alone for any extended period of time.

If you cannot solve the problem any other way, try putting an ad in the paper or hiring a student or older person to look after your bird daily for a fee. Try to make arrangements to find a reliable person in good time. If worse comes to worst, call an animal protection society. The people there may not be able to help you out themselves, but they will help you arrange a solution.

There is one more point I would like to mention: What will happen to the cockatiel if its human partner dies? Remember your cockatiel in your will and indicate what you wish to happen to the animal in that case. An animal protection society will probably provide the best solution, and you may want to support this institution now by taking out a membership.

43

Cockatiels Producing Offspring

Cockatiels become sexually mature at about eight months, but they are not good parents until at least one year old. Younger birds will sometimes start a brood, but they are still too clumsy and undeveloped to keep the baby birds alive. If you have a very young pair, then, you should remove the eggs that may have been laid on the bottom of the cage and wait for the birds to reach a "marriageable age" before putting up nesting boxes. If a pair that is ready to breed has no nesting box, it will try to sit on the eggs on the floor of the cage or some other inappropriate spot with sad results. The hatchlings usually die within a few hours or days.

(If you have a single female, you should remove the eggs, too, which she will lay every few months.)

How Two Birds Become a Couple

If you introduce a new bird into the life of one you have been keeping singly, the two have to adjust to this new situation and develop a mutual sympathy. You will soon notice that the female dominates, even if she asserts herself only gently. She has first choice for a sleeping place, and she will drive the male from the food dish if she wishes to eat. Depending on her mood, she will insist on distance or urge him imperiously to scratch her head if that is her desire. If the male is not still in the playful and rash stage of young adolescence, he will respect the wishes of his future mate.

Gradually a peaceful familiarity will settle in between the two, because male cockatiels by nature never force their will on the female. They have an instinctual inhibition for aggression on which the female relies totally without herself developing any such inhibitions.

Birds that live together also influence each other's moods. If one is preening itself, for instance, the other will also start grooming its feathers; if one assumes a resting position, so will

the other; and if one starts to eat or drink, the other will not be far behind. Even birds that are kept singly will start eating the moment their human "flock companions" sit down to a meal in the same room.

In nature, many birds can forage for food on the ground at the same time. But in a cage, where there is only one dish with seeds, one water dish, and one little rack with pieces of apple, the male is often at a serious disadvantage in satisfying his appetites. I therefore give my birds everything in duplicate in their cage, and they seem to be very happy that way.

Two birds will have to have spent some time together and had sufficient opportunity to do things together—both inside the cage and outside—before habit develops into affection, and affection into love.

Courtship Displays

Before you let nature take its course, reflect once more on the fact that the baby birds will be as much your responsibility as are the parents. Will you want to keep them all? This is first of all a matter of space, because further breeding would be likely, and it also would require a considerable increase in expenditure of time and money.

If you are unable to keep the young birds yourself, ask yourself ahead of time whether you know enough people who would like to take one of the young birds. You will want to entrust them only to homes where you know they will be well taken care of.

If you decide against raising cockatiels, all you need do is to not provide a nesting box and to remove the eggs as they appear.

But back to the topic of courtship displays: In the course of a few months, the male bird, while showing all due respect to the female, will gain more self-assurance and, knowing the limits he must not overstep, will woo his partner more and

44

Cockatiels Producing Offspring

more. Patiently and devotedly, he will scratch her head, and he will try to draw her attention by loudly drumming with his beak on a hard surface or by whistling melodiously and rhythmically with his wings slightly spread. He will also display entirely new flying skills because flying has become an end in itself. The male flies around the room in shallow loops and, with artful maneuvers, keeps changing directions frequently. Finally he will trip around his bride several times in a row with raised crest and slightly raised and spread wings while emitting short, restrained sounds. Then he lowers his head at a slight angle, raises his widely spread tail, and whistles in a loud voice.

Even though the female watches his activities with apparent disinterest, she will get gradually — or suddenly — stimulated sexually, and without any special preliminaries will offer herself to the male by crouching down slightly in a horizontal position and pointing her tail to the side. The male climbs on the female while holding on loosely with his beak to her back feathers or pulling on them and crosses his tail feathers with those of the female in such a way that their cloacas touch (Figure 23). When the cock thus "treads" the hen,

as the copulation of birds is described, male sperm enters the female's cloaca, and the eggs get fertilized. However, we do not know for sure whether all the eggs of a clutch get fertilized together or only one at a time.

During the union of the two, which lasts only a few seconds, the cockatiels emit a soft, singing clucking or quiet squeaks, and the male sometimes produces a purring, apparently reassuring, growl. Then both birds vigorously shake themselves and start preening themselves elaborately.

The Proper Nesting Box

At this point you have to provide a nesting box. You can build one yourself or buy one ready-made. If you decide to construct it yourself, use well-seasoned wood so the walls will not get warped by inside temperatures, and do not bring the box into the bird room until it has stopped smelling of glue. For cockatiels either a tall, narrow box or a wider one can be used. I personally prefer the wider shape because then the entry hole does not have to be located directly over the nesting hollow. This makes the parent birds climb onto the eggs more slowly, and the keeper can check on things more easily.

A nesting box of this kind should have the following dimensions (Figure 24): floor and cover should measure 10 × 15 inches (26 × 38 cm), and the height should be 12 inches (30 cm). On one side of the front wall, in the upper third, make an entry hole about 3 inches (8 cm) in diameter, and almost 2 inches (4 cm) below that attach a landing perch or board. In the bottom board, which should be twice as thick as the sides and cover, a circular nest hollow about 5 inches (12 cm) in diameter has to be carved out so that the eggs will not roll away. The top should flip open to facilitate nest checks, but it should fit on the side walls tightly. For a tall, narrow nesting box, the bottom and top should be about 11 × 11

Figure 23 *Copulation lasts only a few seconds in cockatiels.*

47

Cockatiels Producing Offspring

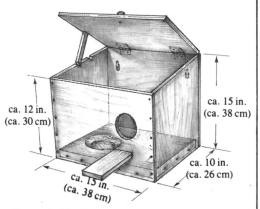

ca. 12 in.
(ca. 30 cm)

ca. 15 in.
(ca. 38 cm)

ca. 10 in.
(ca. 26 cm)

ca. 15 in.
(ca. 38 cm)

Entry hole 3 in. (8 cm)

Figure 24   A nesting box you can build yourself. It has a lid that can be raised, a landing board, an entry hole, a nest hollow, and secure hooks for hanging up.

inches (28 × 28 cm) and the height 15 inches (38 cm). Attach a piece of wire mesh on the inside back wall opposite the entry hole to help the birds climb up and down. But make sure the edges are covered so that the fledglings will not get hurt on them.
Hang the box on a wall in a spot where the birds spend much of their time and where it is readily accessible from both the climbing tree and the cage. Attach some sturdy rings on the back of the box into which equally sturdy hooks that are mounted solidly on the wall fit. Now hang up the nesting box at a convenient height that permits you to look into it easily. When the nesting box is first put up, the birds will examine it suspiciously from a distance, as they do everything new. But soon the female will start approaching it, and when her laying period begins, she will lay her four to six – sometimes as many as nine – eggs in it at two-day intervals. Each egg is laid at the same time of day.

Sitting on the Eggs

When there are two eggs (each weighing 5 to 7 grams) in the nest, the two parents start taking turns sitting on them. Cockatiels share in this parental duty, as do cockatoos, but this behavior has been observed in no other member of the Australian parrot family. The female sits on the eggs during the night, and in the morning the male relieves her, staying on the nest until afternoon. During the 18- to 20-day incubation period both birds are sometimes in the nest, and both leave it together occasionally if they want to eat or drink or relieve themselves, or if they feel like stretching their legs and wings or preening themselves.
The brooding proceeds best if the birds are disturbed or startled as little as possible. Before dusk falls or before you turn the lights off, make sure the female is in the nest box because she will not find her way there in the dark. As a safety measure you should leave a 15-watt bulb on in the room at night so that the birds can always orient themselves easily. And you can make sure the eggs will not get too dry by turning on an air humidifier.
Caution: Do no set out open containers of water; the parent birds could drown in them. If you want to set out water, make sure you cover the containers.
Check the nest about every five days. An egg may have broken, and in that case you should remove it and clean all traces of it off the other eggs. Even very tame cockatiels become aggressive when you approach their nest. Choose a moment, therefore, when both parents are not too close. They will then watch your doings anxiously but will not hack at you in defense of the nest.
If you happen to raise the top of the nesting box while one of the parent birds is sitting, you will be surprised at their violent reaction. With wide open beak they will hiss threateningly at you while rocking back and forth with partly unfolded wings.

Cockatiels Producing Offspring

While the birds are brooding you should feed them a special diet for raising chicks that includes all the important food elements. You can supplement this with hard-boiled egg mixed with zwieback crumbs or with bread soaked in milk and mixed with cottage cheese and with lots of sprouted seeds. Make sure the food is never refrigerator cold and that it does not sit around too long because protein-rich foods spoil quickly. Offer plenty of spray millet, too. If you accustom the parents in good time to the new elements in their diet, the good nutrition of the baby birds will be assured.

The Hatching of the Young

About twenty days after the cockatiels started incubation the young will start to hatch in the order in which the eggs were laid. Now it is especially important to check on the nest but you have to do so cautiously. Every other day you should clean out as much of the droppings as you can from the box because cockatiels, unlike many songbirds, do not keep their nests clean. It can also happen that a hatchling dies and has to be removed. During the first few days your inspections will reveal a tangle of small bird bodies and limbs among which some whole eggs are still visible. Eventually the last one will hatch and be buried underneath its bigger nest mates. Initially, the heads of the baby birds are too heavy to be raised and rest on the ground. The large eyes, though visible, are still completely covered by the lids, and yellow down covers the backs and undersides of the baby birds, leaving the backs of the heads bare, however. Newly hatched baby cockatiels are about 1 1/4 inches (3 cm) long and weigh about 4 to 5 grams. By the time they are three weeks old they weigh about 60 grams (2 ounces). When they leave the nest at four and a half weeks they weigh around 80 grams (almost 3 ounces), which is close to the adult weight. During this

period they undergo an amazing development. The first ten to twelve days the parents feed them almost continually and keep them under their wings. During this time their appearance changes rapidly. After the eleventh day, the claws and feet that were a pinkish flesh color turn bluish. The ceres start darkening, the tip of the beak gets brownish, and after another four days, the entire beak is gray and hard. On the fourth day the eyes already begin to open, and by the tenth day they are fully open. At about the same time the hatchling loses its egg tooth. After the tenth day, the first feather quills become visible, and between the seventeenth day and the twenty-first days the first yellow plumage is replaced by gray down. After eighteen days, there is a suggestion of what will later become the bright red cheek spot; and the feathers of the crest, though still sheathed, rise up at times of excitement. At the age of four weeks, juvenile cockatiels resemble adult females in appearance, and after the first complete molt, which occurs five to nine months after hatching, the young cockatiels display the sexual color differentiations of adult birds.

From their tenth day on, the nestlings can hiss in warning when they are bothered, the way their parents do, and a short time later they spit, raise their miniature crests, spread their little wings, and rock back and forth when angered. Soon after that they will start pecking at the hand of the caretaker. After four and a half to five weeks, one after the other of the young birds leaves the nest for good. At first they merely sit on the ground and still let the parents feed them.

Raising the Young Birds

Now you should set up a play area for the young birds underneath the nesting box. Spread some sand on the floor of the room, or place the young birds into a cage right away, but make sure they get enough opportunity to practice flying. If you

Cockatiels Producing Offspring

place them in an aviary, stick some branches in the wire mesh so the birds recognize it as a boundary and do not crash into it. In a room it is almost unavoidable that the birds bump into a wall and tumble down on their first trial flights because they do not slow down in time. Luckily their speed is usually too slow for them to hurt themselves seriously. Still, it is a good idea to mount a few solid branches firmly around the room to serve as landing perches. A cage is too small in any case for four to six — sometimes even up to eight — young birds. Each bird also needs enough room on a perch or branch to build up its flight muscles by rapidly flapping its wings. If you have a room for the birds, you can stretch thick electrical cable at different heights for this purpose during the first few weeks.

As late as two weeks after leaving the nest, the young birds still beg for food with certain vocalizations while bending down low in front of the parent. At this point they are capable of feeding themselves, but they continue to beg, and their parents respond. No earlier than three weeks after leaving the nesting box but before the parents start a new brood, the young birds should be separated from their parents. Life will be rather chaotic in the room with the birds in the period after the young leave the nesting box, and this time will require extra work and worry for you, but you will remember it with special fondness.

Some crises may arise in this period that you will want to know how to cope with. If one of the parent birds dies after the young have hatched, the surviving partner will feed the young and keep them warm by him- or herself. If this lone parent leaves the nest too long or too often, you have to try to supply some extra warmth (point an infrared or strong electric bulb at the nesting box). If the baby birds do not get enough food, you can try to feed them yourself with a syringe you can buy at a drugstore. Cover the tip with a piece of small rubber tubing to avoid injuring the delicate pharynxes of the young birds. Now prepare a mixture

of babyfood, mashed, hard-boiled egg yolk, grated carrot, and some minced parsley or chickweed and squeeze some of it into each of the beaks about every two hours. Later on you can use a small spoon and somewhat coarser foods.

You may run into another problem. After all the young birds have left the nesting box, you have to observe them carefully. It sometimes happens that one of them is somewhat neglected by the parents. This bird will seem apathetic and have difficulty flying or not attempt to do so at all. Even though such a disadvantaged bird will not look sick — it will not fluff up its feathers — you should grab it gently and try to feed it. In many cases, such a bird will have caught up with the others within a few days.

Special Chapter:
Understanding Cockatiels

The Family

The following schema is meant to help you locate cockatiels in the family of birds. Of course, this is nothing more than an excerpt, because a full classification would fill many pages.

I.   Class: Birds (Aves)
II. Order: Parrots and allies (Psittaciformes)
III. Family: Parrots (Psittacidae)

According to K. Kolar in Grzimek's *Animal Life (Tierleben)*, the family of parrots is subdivided into 7 subfamilies, 75 genera, and 326 species with 816 subspecies.

IV. Subfamilies:
   1. Kea and Kaka (Nestorinae)
   2. Pesquet's Parrot (Psittrichasinae)
   3. Cockatoos (Cacatuinae)
   4. Pygmy parrots (Micropsittinae)
   5. Lories and Lorikeets (Trichoglossinae)
   6. Owl Parrot or Kakapo (Strigopinae)
   7. All other parrots (Psittacinae)

The subfamily Psittacinae is further subdivided into the following tribes:
   a. Wedge-tailed parrots (Araini), among which are the macaws.
   b. Blunt-tailed parrots (Psittacini), including the well-known amazons and African gray parrots.
   c. Wax-billed parrots (Loriini), among which are the ringneck parakeets and the lovebirds.
   d. Hanging parakeets (Loriculini) with only a few species.
   e. Rosellas and allies (Platycercini), including the budgerigars, Australian grass parakeets, night parrots, ground parrots, and rosellas. Many ornithologists class the cockatiels with the rosellas (genus *Platycercus*).

The Anatomy of a Cockatiel

The cockatiel *(Nymphicus hollandicus)* is a medium-sized bird, measuring $11\frac{1}{2}$–$13\frac{1}{2}$ inches (29–34 cm) from the beak to the tip of the tail and weighing 80–100 grams. Almost half of the length is taken up by the tail feathers with—typical for this species—the feathers getting longer from the side to the middle and making the tail look like a long platter when viewed from the side. Both mandibles are curved in parrot fashion and are powerful, with the upper one being hinged to the skull. The nostrils are located in the ceres at the base of the upper mandible. Like most parrots, cockatiels have strong legs and a zygodactyl arrangement of the toes, which means that two toes point forward and two backward. Their prehensile feet are responsible for the climbing dexterity of parrots and for the habit many species have of holding onto food and other objects while working them over with the bill.

To be able to talk easily with bird experts such as pet dealers and veterinarians, it is helpful to know something about your bird's anatomy and what the different parts of the body are called. This is why we have provided the schematic picture of a cockatiel (Figure 25).

The Five Senses

Sense of Smell
We know only little about the workings and efficiency of the *sense organs* of birds, but obser-

51

Special Chapter: Understanding Cockatiels

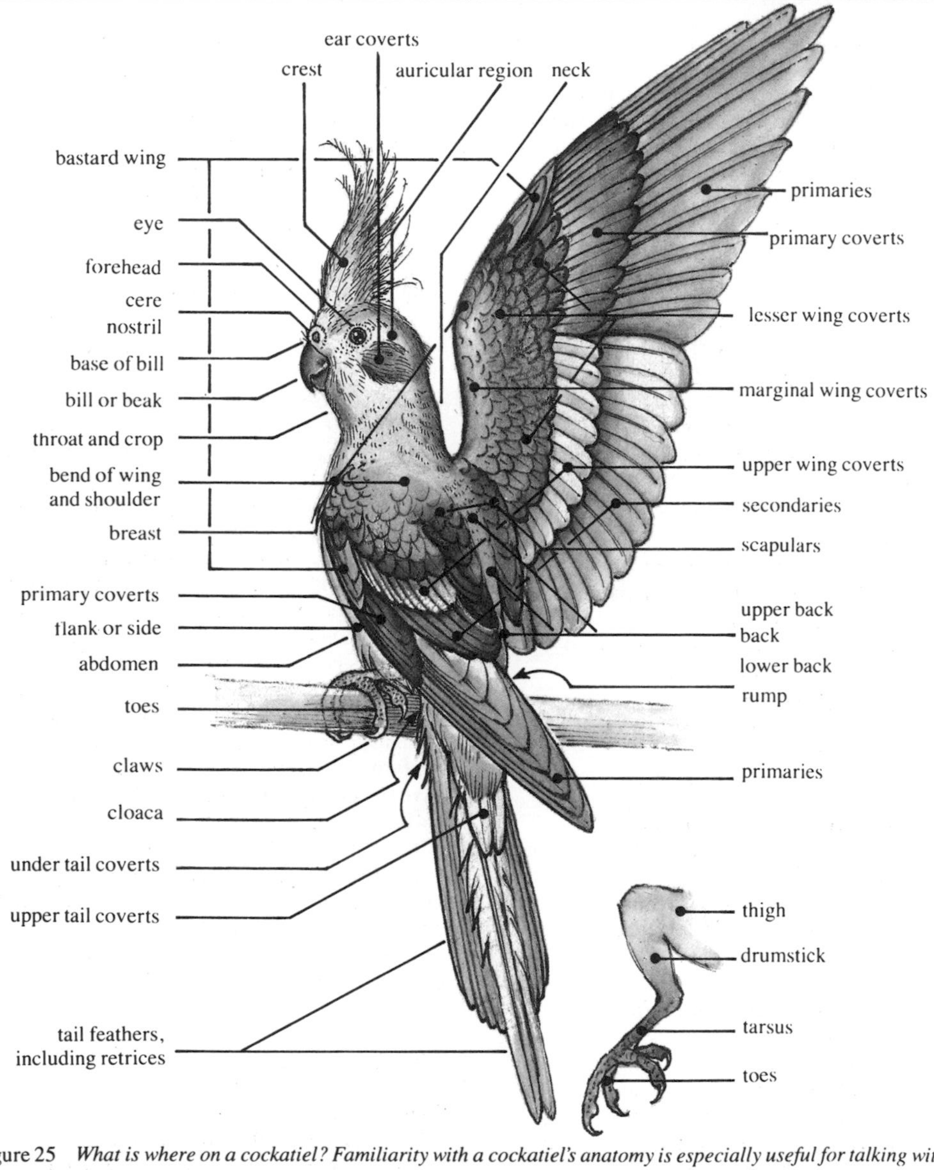

Figure 25 *What is where on a cockatiel? Familiarity with a cockatiel's anatomy is especially useful for talking with the veterinarian.*

vation shows that cockatiels associate positive and negative impressions with specific smells. It has been noticed, for example, that even moderate concentrations of smoke and chemical odors cause cockatiels to become restless and to emit characteristic sounds of fear.

Sense of Touch

The *tactile sensitivities* of cockatiels are adapted to life in the outdoors. Feet and legs are relatively insensitive, and especially the bottoms of the toes react practically not at all to contact with rough surfaces and pointed or sharp objects. If the upper side of the toes is touched, however, the birds respond by pulling back the foot. The birds withdraw or retreat from anything that threatens to hold them fast or obstruct flight.

The tongue of a cockatiel is an extremely sensitive organ of touch. With it the bird investigates food and objects, checks the condition of plumage and skin, and determines what is useful and what is not, what is harmful and what is safe. The skin reacts with equal sensitivity to the preening done by a partner. If the partner providing the service does so clumsily, touching a sensitive spot or probing newly sprouting quills too early, the "mistreated" party jerks back, emits a brief cry of protest, and hacks at the partner in warning.

Sense of Taste

The tongue does not do much in the way of tasting because the variety of food available in the cockatiel's natural habitat is extremely limited. The fledglings learn from their parents what is good to eat, and, depending on what experience brings their way, they may expand the range of what they consider edible in the course of later life. Taste does play a certain role because unwholesome or poisonous substances that have not already been eliminated by the tongue with its tactile abilities can be detected by taste. Cockatiels that are kept as pets in fact develop quite pronounced likes and dislikes in the area of food, and

there is one liking that all pet birds share: a passion for salt. This probably has something to do with the fact that the diet of birds held in captivity can never be the same as that offered by a natural habitat, where no doubt salty substances are present in plants and in the soil. So if your bird occasionally nibbles on a salt lick or a pretzel do not worry. It is probably making up for a slight deficiency in its diet.

Sense of Hearing

The hearing of cockatiels is excellent but it is not in a league with that of dogs. Birds hear sounds in the same frequencies that are audible to humans, and they distinguish between familiar and unfamiliar sounds, to which they react with fright, fear, curiosity, or pleasure. Many cockatiels like music and show a special predilection for the sound of certain instruments. My cockatiels Toni and Wutzi, for instance, love violin concerts and snuggle up happily to the loudspeaker while the music lasts. Other birds get used to vacuum cleaners and accompany it with sounds of their own invented especially for this situation. Again others learn to recognize the slamming of a car door or the opening of the apartment door and quite correctly associate it with the return of a favorite person.

Sense of Sight

For many birds, sight is the best developed of the five senses. This is especially true of cockatiels. They love to survey the world from an elevated perch because their excellent eyesight guarantees them the best protection against enemies. This inborn habit often causes them discomfort in their lives as pets in a home because they notice any slight change and often respond to harmless goings-on with fear and flight reactions. On the other hand, all changes also evoke their curiosity. They eye unfamiliar objects, new surroundings, or strange people intently and with crest erect. Even very tame cockatiels that are

Special Chapter: Understanding Cockatiels

used to living with people shy away from strangers not only on first meeting them but sometimes treat them with distrust for weeks. But they will turn to the familiar caretaker without the slightest hesitation or fear as soon as that person reappears. Even a familiar person can put them in a minor panic if he or she turns up in unaccustomed garb or drastically changed in some other way. On the other hand, cockatiels can also have "friends," i.e., recognize people or other animals as safe and worthy of trust, even though these friends are not around all the time and the birds may see them only rarely. The same pattern holds for unfamiliar surroundings, as when you take your cockatiel somewhere else when you go away on vacation. Here, too, the first visit will trigger fear that gradually subsides while at later occasions things will begin to look familiar, and the bird will soon feel at home again.

Figure 26 *The strong, curved upper mandible of a cockatiel is hinged to the skull; the shorter lower mandible is connected solidly.*

Agility and Preening

Cockatiels are not only one of the most agile and fastest fliers among Australian parakeets, but they are also great climbers. With their toes — two of which point forward and two back — and the aid of powerful beaks, they can accomplish feats a rock climber would envy. By craning the neck forward and grabbing hold with the beak, then pulling first one and then the other leg after them, they can get themselves across wide spans where other birds would have to resort to their wings. Cockatiels can also swivel their heads 180° so that by turning their heads they can scan the world all the way around.

Thanks to the acrobatic mobility of all parts of the body, a cockatiel can reach everywhere with its bill to groom its plumage. It leaves only the head and neck feathers to the ministrations of its partner or, in a pinch, works them over itself with its toes. Preening takes up a good part of a bird's time, and in the course of it each of the thousands of feathers is carefully drawn through the bill, smoothed out and freed of dust in the process, and then oiled again. The entire length of even the long wing and tail feathers slides through the bill, often causing the birds to strike up the most artful poses. In the course of preening, the bird repeatedly picks up oil from the preen gland with its bill. The oil keeps the feathers elastic and water-repellent. The head is greased by rubbing it and moving it back and forth over the preen gland, which is located

Figure 27 *To scratch its head, a cockatiel does not reach up directly with its foot but instead raises it between the wing and the body.*

54

on the lower back just above the spot where the tail feathers sprout.

When scratching its head, a cockatiel raises the scratching leg between the body and the wing (Figure 27), a peculiarity it shares with many other kinds of birds including a number of parrots and even some songbirds. Just what this method of scratching represents in the evolutionary history of birds is still debated by ornithologists. Some see it as a relic from the distant days when evolution separated birds from reptiles, a claim that others dismiss since there are some nestlings that scratch by raising the leg straight forward while their parents adhere to the leg between body and wing posture.

Sounds and Calls as Evidence of Intelligence

If you spend a lot of time with your cockatiel and observe it carefully, you will learn to understand much of what a bird can express by means of body language and sounds. Above all you will soon be able to tell when your bird wants some specific thing, when it is happy, what it is afraid of, and when it feels lonely and needs special attention. Cockatiels are intelligent and display amazing patterns of behavior, some of them innate, others learned.

A careful observer with a good ear will soon realize how varied the calls are. While a lonely bird will screech madly at an unpleasantly high decibel level, a contented cockatiel will make use of the limited modulations its voice is capable of to make itself understood at what could be described as a reasonable tone. The familiar figure who takes care of it, as well as other people and animals it knows, are greeted with a happy cry while their departure evokes a rather resigned note. I know a young woman with a pair of cockatiels who sometimes has two cats visiting her apartment. The birds show not the slightest fear

of the cats and watch them with pleasure from their cage (the birds are not left alone in the room with the cats). When the cats lose interest in the birds and move away, both cockatiels break out in sounds of protest that are much louder than their usual talk.

It is also worth mentioning that many cockatiels will answer when they are called. The bird whose name has been called will respond either with the sound paired birds use to communicate with each other when they perch on different branches or with a special whistle a bird that is kept singly has learned for this purpose from its caretaker. Cockatiels are also very quick to recognize when their favorite person is getting ready to leave the room. A cockatiel that lives free in the room will then quickly fly to the person's shoulder with a special call used at these occasions.

The conversation of a bonded pair of cockatiels consists primarily of calls from one partner to the other to join him or her. They call to each other mostly when they find themselves sitting on different perches, which seems to them to be an unnatural state of affairs. Usually the male keeps calling until the female joins him. If she hesitates at all, the male immediately goes to get her, sounding his call the whole time. When the pair is together the birds understand each other without vocalizations. The male always leads in any activity. He is the one to try out landing sites and to check out unfamiliar objects to see if they are dangerous or useful. In the latter case he demonstrates to his partner by ostentatiously taking possession and by repeated calls that he has discovered something new. He is also the one to threaten, hiss, and sometimes even bite in a dangerous situation while she withdraws behind him, threatening and hissing only reluctantly.

Single birds living in close contact with humans, of course, have much more opportunity to display their intelligence in the daily interaction with them. They get used to daily routines and learn to connect certain causes with their effects. My

Special Chapter: Understanding Cockatiels

cockatiel Koko, for instance, knew exactly what a dictaphone is for. He knew how to whistle not only "Lightly Row" but also a special little tune of his own that he would repeat over and over for about twenty times at the same pitch. When on our screened-in balcony, he often whistled this sequence of notes out of pure joie de vivre. But as soon as I would start to dictate into the microphone of the tape recorder, Koko would immediately fly to my desk and drown out my voice with his, and my secretaries would later complain laughingly of this sound interference.

Wutzi, Toni's partner, shows his intelligence in a different way. When the birds have to return to their cage, all I need to do with Toni is to extend the back of my hand. She knows that she will be put into the cage when she sits on my hand but she patiently submits whereas the somewhat more obstinate Wutzi will retreat to a tall shelf or a lamp. When I am in a hurry I simply pick up the cage with Toni in it and go toward the door saying "Good-bye, Wutzi. Toni and I are leaving." Then Wutzi comes flying instantly to the cage with a typical cry of fear, asking to be let in. Obviously, the thought of being left alone is more than he can bear.

Activities, Moods, Reactions

The crest of feathers that cockatiels have serves as a good indicator of mood. If the crest is raised on the top of the head with the tip pointing slightly backward, this means that the bird is active, enterprising, interested in what is going on, and ready either to turn to its partner or to show itself off while whistling and slightly raising its wings. If there is no partner to groom, it may gently nibble the hand of a person it knows well. If not enough attention and affection are forthcoming, it may resort to some display activities to elicit the desired appreciation. With wings slightly extended it will – as when wooing a mate – circle in small

Figure 28   Left: *A normally raised crest indicates that the cockatiel is curious and ready for action.* Right: *An almost horizontal crest means that the bird is in a contemplative mood.*

Figure 29   Left: *A rigidly raised crest with the tips of the feathers pointing forward indicates that the bird is extremely agitated and ready to defend itself.* Right: *If excitement and aggression lead to actual attack and spitting or to fearful retreat, the crest is quickly folded down but is so tense that even the tips of the feathers stick out straight to the back.*

Figure 30   Left: *If the bird is terrified, the tips of the crest feathers curve slightly upward and quiver.* Right: *Once the excitement has passed and calm returns, the crest resumes its normal horizontal position.*

Special Chapter: Understanding Cockatiels

steps and then bow its body forward with spread wings and raised tail, never for a moment taking its eyes off the person it is trying to impress.

Other activities include flying around and frequently changing from one high perch to another, trying out less familiar landing sites, and nibbling on wallpaper, protruding edges, and plants. As its interest slackens or the period of activity comes to a close, giving way to a more relaxed and peaceful mood, the crest is folded down almost horizontally, and only the tips of the feathers stick up at the back of the head. In this frame of mind, cockatiels like to indulge in thorough preening and in working over the legs and toes with the bill. At the conclusion of preening, first one leg and then the other is stretched far back and finally both wings are raised straight up. These stretching exercises can also signal a renewed phase of activity after a period of rest.

If the bird succumbs to drowsiness after a spell of quiet, it tucks its bill in the lightly fluffed feathers on the back, closes its eyes, ceases to take notice of what is going on, and goes to sleep. If it is a deep sleep, one leg is usually raised and buried in the belly feathers.

If the crest stands straight up with the tips of the feathers pointing almost forward, this is a sign that the cockatiel is extremely excited or nervous. Perhaps something unfamiliar has both startled it and aroused its curiosity, putting it in a state of tense alertness, or perhaps it is fearlessly hissing and threatening a supposed enemy. This kind of total attention that involves all the senses is exhausting and can be maintained only for a few seconds. That is why the moment of tense immobility gives way quickly to physical maneuvers of reaction. If possible, the bird will try to make its escape, or it will withdraw, cowering in a corner of the cage, and watch from there what is going on. Perhaps it will realize that the commotion giving rise to its excitement was harmless, and it will start eating or simply move to a different place. But if the fear-inspiring situation persists,

the bird's fright will keep intensifying. The crest is lowered as though calm has returned, but the tips of the feathers tremble lightly. Now the bird will hiss threateningly with head tilted back, and it will respond by hacking if its flight path is obstructed or if the partner or the nest are in danger and must be defended.

Just as the shape of the crest changes smoothly from one to another of the postures described, so do the moods shift back and forth almost imperceptibly. The only obvious sign of a change in mood is when a bird shakes off previous tension, whether brought on by positive or negative causes. The bird then literally shakes itself from head to tail (Figure 31) so that one can hear the feathers rustle. If there is a minor irritation, caused by unpleasant though familiar noises, bright light, or activities it does not approve of, the bird will react with a light twitching of the facial feathers, a reaction that is unique to cockatiels.

If you have a pair of cockatiels, you will notice that their moods are synchronized. Fear and excitement, curiosity and drowsiness, the desire to eat, drink, or preen its own or the partner's plumage — all these moods immediately communicate themselves from one partner to the other.

Figure 31 *Cockatiels literally "shake off" the tension and agitation of a previous mood.*

59

Special Chapter: Understanding Cockatiels

Often the two birds will execute the same movements at the same moment or strike the same pose, giving the impression of going through a well-rehearsed performance. As a rule, the two birds live in complete harmony and whatever misunderstandings arise are disposed of with a quick threatening posture or the suggestion of hacking at each other. A subsequent shake of the feathers completely clears up whatever trouble there was.

Keep in mind, if you have a single bird, how much this gentle creature will miss a partner. It will try as much as possible to make up for this lack by accommodating to you, resting when you are sitting quietly and eating when you are having your meals in the same room or are whistling, singing, or talking. You are also the only one who can satisfy your cockatiel's desire for mutual grooming by gently scratching its head and neck and wherever else it seems to enjoy it when it is in the right mood and submits to it with obvious pleasure. If your finger scares it, try the tip of your nose! But do not startle it with rough petting against the lie of the feathers. No bird likes that. Feel your way carefully to the base of the feathers and then pet sideways, gradually progressing to the next higher row of feathers.

The Natural Habitat of Cockatiels

Cockatiels favor open grounds and avoid dense forests. They find food, congenial surroundings, and nesting sites in open savannas with eucalyptus trees, in brush steppes, and in desertlike areas with tough grasses. Their favorite areas are along creeks that carry water only at certain times of the year.

Because of the climatic conditions of their native Australian habitat, cockatiels are used to dry heat. The peak temperatures in the middle of the day range from 86°–113°F (30°–45°C), and at night it may get to below freezing. A slow drop in temperature therefore does no harm to cockatiels, but rapid drops can result in sickness and death. During the hot part of the day, cockatiels rest, which lowers the need for oxygen and reduces the evaporation of body moisture. In the cooler morning and afternoon hours, the birds travel long distances in search of food and water. During the dry periods they feed exclusively on dry grass and herbaceous seeds. Along with the seeds, the birds pick up some coarse sand, which helps the process of digestion. Cockatiels have also been observed in flowering trees and shrubs, where they feed on the nectar of the flowers and on small insects. Cockatiels seem to have a greater need for water than some other Australian parrots, frequenting watering spots every one to three hours. Since cockatiels are always uneasy on the ground, they drink hastily, often barely alighting to do so, and bathe only rarely. But when it rains they like to hang head down from tall branches with their wings fully extended and enjoy showering in the rain.

Cockatiels fly in a straight line and very fast at great heights while emitting a call that sounds like "queel-queel." The flocks stick closely together, the white wing bands apparently serving as optical signals. Observers often express surprise at their sudden, vertical landing. The birds let themselves drop, slow their fall just above the ground, and land quickly. When they are foraging on the ground, the slightest disturbance will make them rise up in a panic and retreat to high trees and bushes preferably with dead limbs. There the gray color of their plumage serves as camouflage against the gray of the dead wood, and the great field of vision from this height gives them a sense of security. The cockatiels' only defense against predators is flight, and they are indeed one of the fastest fliers of all parakeets.

The natural predators of cockatiels are predators birds. Cockatiels are used to danger coming from above, which is why they seek out exposed perches from which they can see far. This means

Special Chapter: Understanding Cockatiels

unfortunately that they provide an easy target for cats because they are not by nature equipped with defense reactions against enemies that creep up on the ground. Cockatiels also acquired an enemy, though not one that is after their lives, in the starlings *(Sturnus vulgaris)* imported in the 1850s and 1860s. These birds compete with the peaceful cockatiels for nesting sites and will emerge victorious even if the cockatiels are already brooding a complete clutch.

How Cockatiels Live in Nature

The mating and brooding period of most birds is determined by the length of daylight hours, but the nomadic cockatiels of inland Australia are not bound by the cycle of the seasons. The hormonal changes that give rise to display behavior and readiness to mate occur in cockatiels whenever a rainy period starts or when the birds in the course of their nomadic wanderings find themselves in an area that has recently had prolonged rainfalls. Then the usually desiccated vegetation is awakened by the rain to new growth. Only after significant rainfalls can cockatiels find enough ripening seeds and young growth and for a long enough period to raise their young. They seem to have secret antennae for these conditions because they often start the preliminaries of breeding well before the rains start.

In the breeding areas there is much lively activity at such times. Pairs of cockatiels are on the lookout for suitable nesting sites which may have to be expanded or have the entry holes enlarged. Hollows in dead tree limbs as far off the ground as possible are preferred because the birds need to be able to survey the surrounding terrain while they brood. The bottom of the hollow is not elaborately prepared. At most the debris from expanding the cavity accumulates in the bottom. No nesting material in the proper sense of the word is used.

Cockatiels share their breeding grounds with budgerigars and cockatoos, each species seeking out the nesting sites that suit it. The general hustle and bustle stimulates display activity and readiness to mate in all the birds, and in each nest four to seven eggs, having been laid at two-day intervals generally in the morning, will be ready in good time, often before the rain even starts. After the three weeks that the incubation takes, the rain has revived the vegetation sufficiently so that there is enough rearing food available. The parent birds, too, benefit from the diet of half-ripe seeds and sprouting plants that are so rich in vitamins and proteins. During the brooding time the male sits on the eggs during the day and the female during the night. The bird that is not sitting uses the time off to seek food for itself and to keep a close watch on the nesting site. After the baby birds hatch, both parents spend all their time for the next five weeks feeding them. The nest is not kept clean as it is in the case of some other birds, but nature provides for adequate hygiene. There are some small butterfly larvae that live in the nesting cavities and feed on the hatchlings' droppings.

The parents still look after and feed the young cockatiels for a few weeks after they leave the nest. But when the mother bird starts laying a new clutch of eggs, the earlier batch of offspring is left more and more to take care of itself. By then the birds have reached adult size, wear juvenile plumage, and are completely fit to live the life of a cockatiel in the wild. One major difference between captive and wild cockatiels is that the latter do not reach sexual maturity until their second year, a whole year later than birds that are reared in captivity. There is a good reason for this prolonged adolescence. A flock of cockatiels remains in a given rearing ground as long as the food supply lasts, raising a second and sometimes even a third brood there if possible. Only when the vegetation becomes exhausted do the birds move on in small flocks — not strictly together as families — to other areas where they mingle with other small flocks. There the young birds have a chance to meet and select unrelated mates of their own age.

Cockatiels know each other personally; i.e., each bird in a flock recognizes the others as individuals. Males and females consequently do not pair up haphazardly, but pairs bond well ahead of mating season out of affection for each other and remain faithful to each other for life. Mutual grooming is the outward display of this affection. During the breeding season the pairs leave the flock and live by themselves. When the business of rearing young is done, the pairs return to the flock but remain bonded. Only the death of a partner can cause a bird to look for a new mate. But in any case the pairing is based on personal sympathy. Cockatiels also feel antipathy toward others of their kind, and such feelings would always stand in the way of pairing up. Someone might object that this cannot be true because this phenomenon is rarely observed in captivity where birds are often paired arbitrarily without reacting with rejection and aggression. To this I would respond with the example of two people stranded on an island. The two may not like each other but they will make do with each other, get used to each other, and relieve the solitude for each other. If cockatiels are kept in large community aviaries, it becomes quite clear that they respond with differentiated feelings to each other and select their mates on the basis of these feelings.

Useful Addresses

American Cockatiel Society
9812 Bois D'Arc Court
Fort Worth, TX 76126 (USA)

American Federation of Aviculture Inc.
P.O. Box 1125
Garden Grove, CA 92642 (USA)

Avicultural Society of America
734 North Highland Avenue
Hollywood, CA 90038 (USA)

Avicultural Society of Australia
P.O. Box 48
Bentleigh East
Victoria (Australia)

Canadian Avicultural Society, Inc.
32 Dromore Crescent
Willowdale 450
Ontario, M2R 2H5 (Canada)

Canadian Institute of Bird Breeders
4422 Chauvin Street
Pierrefonds, Quebec (Canada)

The Avicultural Society
20 Bourbon Street
London W.1 (England)

The New Zealand Federation of Cage Bird Societies
31 Harker Street
Christchurch 2 (New Zealand)

Index